A Touch of Genius

A Touch of Genius

A Hopeful Guide to Parenting a Child with Asperger's

Lily Stamford

ARCHWAY
PUBLISHING

Archway Publishing books may be ordered through booksellers or by contacting:

Archway Publishing
1663 Liberty Drive
Bloomington, IN 47403
www.archwaypublishing.com
1 (888) 242-5904

ISBN: 978-1-4808-7592-0 (sc)
ISBN: 978-1-4808-8111-2 (hc)
ISBN: 978-1-4808-7593-7 (e)

Library of Congress Control Number: 2019903056

Print information available on the last page.

Archway Publishing rev. date: 07/19/2019

Autism doesn't come with a manual. It comes with a parent who never gives up.
—Kerry Magro

Dedicated to the parents who never give up.

Contents

A Note from the Author

While the facts and narrative details in this book are accurate and largely based on real characters, some facts as well as names and locations of individuals, schools, and companies have been changed for the sake of privacy.

Preface

Parents anticipate and prepare for many aspects of child rearing. Raising a child on the autism spectrum, however, is not one of them. While parenting involves learning on the job day by day and week by week, I am writing this book because there are certain lessons that do not need repeating. My goal is to prevent parents, wherever possible, from having to reinvent the wheel of raising a child on the spectrum.

This book is meant as a guide. As such, it is filled with a plethora of recommendations for raising a child on the spectrum, ranging from education to mental health to finances. From my personal experience and the extensive research that went into writing this book, however, my overarching message is that the ultimate success of the child is a function of the complete, unwavering support and advocacy of at least one parent.

I want to share with you lessons learned from my own experience raising my son with Asperger's. I hope it will shed light on and ultimately brighten your journey. I also believe that had I been able to point to a success story when I first learned that my son was on the spectrum, my experience would have been different. If I had had a role model showing me that things could work out, I would have looked at the future more optimistically. I hope my story will fill this gap for all those who read it.

This book is the culmination of what I wish I had known when I first started out. Though I don't believe it is possible to come to terms in advance with the challenges you will face, I believe it is possible to ease the presence of those challenges.

Never in a million years did I think my son would live happily and independently thousands of miles away from me. No one told me this would be possible. More often than not, people told me what they thought would be impossible. I fought the odds, however, and met the challenge. The thousands of emails I wrote, the countless hours I spent on the phone, the meetings, the research, the bone-tiring persistence—were they worth it? Absolutely, yes. Were the hours of anguish and fear worth it? I don't think so.

I spent too much of my time as a parent in a hopeless frantic state, one that I believe is avoidable. Of course, knowing that one person's child with autism has successfully transitioned into an independent life does not mean that you can know what the future holds for your child. All I can really offer you is the little fact that things can work out. In this book I talk about how and when they worked out for us. I also talk about when and how they didn't work out so well for us. And I talk about what new parents can do to improve the likelihood of happiness and productivity for their own child.

It is my hope and intention that this book will open the door for you to the immense possibilities that Asperger's carries.

—Lily Stamford

Acknowledgments

I would like to express my thanks to the mentors and champions who worked with my son, Michael. Thank you to Dr. Daniels. Your wonderful demeanor combined with your complete understanding of Asperger's was beyond important to Michael's success. Thank you to Dr. Masserman, who also shared his expertise and love of music while giving the encouraging nudges Michael needed to be successful. To everyone who cared for Michael, thank you. There were so many people who didn't really seem to understand our difficulties. Those who took the time to ask, to care, to question, to offer help, thank you! Thank you to the most amazing advocate and lawyer who cared about Michael always, fielding calls from me day and night for over 10 years, and intervening when necessary. Thank you specifically to those friends like Rachel, Joanne, and Lucy who were always there coaching me and helping me do research for this book. I wish I could list every one of you, but you know who you are!

Introduction

I felt my phone buzz in my pocket. When I picked it up and saw Michael's name on the screen, I readied myself for the worst. This is one of the habits you develop when your child has Asperger's syndrome[1]. You become constantly available and constantly prepared to manage disaster. One day earlier I had sent my son off on a trip alone from Fairfield, Connecticut, to San Francisco for an interview with Apple. He had graduated from Ivy League school number two a few months prior, but the transition between school and job searching had been uncertain until this series of interviews. I was trying to prepare myself—in all the ways I had learned over the last two decades—to find patience, to process disappointment, and to rebuild a broken Michael. I swiped open the call.

"Michael?"

"Mom, I got the job, and it wasn't even the job I applied for. They offered me a better one."

To use words like *pride* or *love* or even *relief* still feels like an understatement. What words exist to express summiting

---

[1] Asperger's syndrome is not included in the DSM 5, but I will continue to refer to it throughout the book because no replacement terminology has been used to define the high end of the autism spectrum.

a mountain you've been climbing for more than twenty years? How can I talk about achievement without first explaining how deep the bar had been buried for us? Michael had overcome the low expectations that teachers and peers had too often held for him throughout his life, and he had beaten the odds recited to us by even the most optimistic doctors. He had found solutions to his own challenges, and with this news he had surpassed his own belief in himself.

Twenty years ago, I sat in a chair in a doctor's office, my clammy hands fidgeting with one another waiting for the diagnosis: yes or no.

"Your son may never learn to drive," the doctor had said, "and he may never go to college."

Today, my son, Michael, is a data scientist at Apple. He has been there for two and a half years. He lives on his own in a city across the country from his father and me. He excels at his job. He loves his life. This kid is one in a million. What prompted me to write this book, however, is the number of kids like Michael out there who might never be able to realize their own capacity. Asperger's syndrome, along with every place along the autism spectrum, poses a unique set of challenges. It comes with the burden of public bias and misunderstanding, of stereotyping and judgment, but it also comes with an extraordinary mind and quirky, refreshing perspectives on the world. With a strong support system, kids with Asperger's can, and do, excel.

Resources for autism spectrum disorder and for Asperger's syndrome are not as scarce as they were twenty years ago, but they certainly aren't as easy to access as they should be. I hope this book will fill some of the gaps.

Every autism diagnosis is different. Michael's story will not be your child's story. Each kid on the spectrum is different in terms of skills, ambitions, thoughts, and dreams. Many will not attend college or mainstream school. You and I will not parent in the same way. We will, however, share the same burden of unexpected challenges and the rush of unexpected joys.

Any parent with a child on the autism spectrum has been through the disappointment of accepting a new and different reality than the one for which they had hoped. Few, however, have been told about all the possibilities to which they have to look forward. Parents have read lists, they have ticked off boxes, they have willed themselves to acknowledge the telltale signs of autism, which in and of themselves are drenched in stigma: worse than normal eye contact, poor social skills, fewer friends, odd mannerisms—the list goes on. The diagnosis stage is filled with explanations of how your child will suffer more than a neurotypical child. What's too often missing in this stage is the other half of what your child may become. In this book I am focused on the positive side of the story, the opportunity for your child to reach his or her potential.

I want parents to understand that these children are special, and that often they are geniuses. They are the Bill Gates, Steve Jobs, Wozniaks, and Zuckerbergs. They are top doctors, lawyers, surgeons, accountants, actors, and money managers. These kids are the ones who perseverate, who raise their voices, who walk with a different gait, and who speak with an odd lilt. They are the ones who will change the world.

Chapter 1
Diagnosis

As parents, we learn to respond to the call of instinct, regardless of fear or disappointment. One day in early 1995 when Michael was four years old, I reached out to our physician and told her we needed help with our son. John, my husband, and I had been struggling. Instead of feeling that the challenges of having a new child were dissipating, we felt that every month bore new hardships, each more difficult than the last.

Our physician recommended a pediatric psychiatrist at Fairfield Hospital. Dr. Longwood helped us address several issues with Michael, including struggles with impulsivity, rigidity, and ADHD through the use of a Catapres patch and psychotherapy. None of these treatments, however, quite solved the puzzle. Nonetheless, I usually felt better walking out of his office than I had felt walking in. One day, about a year after we started seeing him, this changed. On this particular day, Dr. Longwood seemed quieter than usual and more formal. He gestured for me to have a seat and then told me that he believed Michael might be on the Asperger's continuum.

"The Asperger's continuum?" I didn't know what this meant.

Dr. Longwood pulled out a sheet of paper and drew an x and a y axis. He drew a diagonal line from zero that made steady forward progress equidistant from each axis. This line represented neurotypical development. Then he drew a second line. This line did not share the same forward motion but rather grew farther and farther away from the first as it progressed, slowing as it moved ahead. With Asperger's, Dr. Longwood explained, development will not progress at the same rate as neurotypical development. This second line—the one that was supposed to represent my son—seemed to suggest that individuals with Asperger's would become more and more different over time (maturing on an alternate path) than their peers. I looked over to where Michael was playing in the corner of the office and I wished my instincts would tell me that this doctor was wrong. I wished there wasn't a little voice in my head whispering that this confirmed what I already knew.

It took a couple months to get an official diagnosis—first by seeing a neuropsychology expert who tested Michael and then by finding an Asperger's specialist who could make the final call. It took another year and a half to get Michael into regular visits with this same specialist, Dr. Daniels, whom he would continue to see throughout his childhood and adolescence and into adulthood.

The diagnosis took three appointments with Dr. Daniels. The first was with John, Michael, and me; the second was with Michael alone; and the third, the one when we received the official news, was only for John and me.

Even if you already mostly know, you cannot prepare for when you really know. I knew Michael was hyper. I knew he was loud and not very interested in other kids. But I didn't know it was Asperger's. The truth was, I didn't want the doctor to say the word *Asperger's* or explain it to me. I wanted to go on living our regular lives without this diagnosis.

In retrospect, this was my first lesson in the importance of a support system. It took me years to learn the crucial role finding support would play. In all honesty, it took me too long to learn how to ask for help and where to find it.

Two memories rise from the murk of that meeting: the concreteness of Dr. Daniel's first statement—*"Your son has Asperger's syndrome. He may never drive. He may never go to college"*—and the kind sadness on his face. In that moment, I understood that he was a man weathered by the delivery of bad news.

"How serious is it?" It was the only thing I could think to ask. "Mild, moderate, severe?"

Dr. Daniels looked as if he were trying to make sure his words were finding their way to me. "He has it." He said this slowly, patiently. "Moderate, but he has it."

As soon as I got home that night, I turned to the still new internet. Those were the "trash in, trash out" days, and the information available was sullen at best, horrifying at worst. I found myself looping through the Diagnostic and Statistical Manual for Mental Disorders' (DSM IV) list of symptoms for

Asperger's syndrome.[2] The first symptom listed four subcategories and said that an Asperger's diagnosis required significant impairment in at least two of them. With each of the four items I asked myself, *Does this apply to Michael?*

A. "Marked impairments in the use of multiple nonverbal behaviors such as eye-to-eye gaze, facial expression, body posture, and gestures to regulate social interaction." Check.

B. "Failure to develop peer relationships appropriate to developmental level." Check, but I couldn't help but ask myself how bad were his relationships with his peers really?

C. "A lack of spontaneous seeking to share enjoyment, interest or achievements with other people (e.g. by a lack of showing, bringing, or pointing out objects of interest to other people)." I wasn't so sure about this one.

D. "Lack of social or emotional reciprocity." Sometimes yes, sometimes no.

No matter how many loopholes I found, no matter how many alternative answers I tried to force, I couldn't change the truth. Michael was on the autism spectrum. I had no clue what to do about it and no idea what to expect from the future. The only information I felt I was getting at that time was that life had just gotten a whole lot harder, more confusing, and more painful. No one was there to fill in the hope around the edges, to tell me about all the amazing possible

---

[2] See Appendix 1

outcomes that would make the challenges throughout the journey worth their difficulty. If you are currently sitting where I was then, I hope this guide can be that missing voice for you and your family.

Chapter 2
The Hunt for Resources

The first concrete step forward comes after the diagnosis, when wondering is replaced with action. This is when you realize you know nothing compared with what you must know. You become a seeker and a sponge. So much is inconsistent. Nothing is enough.

A professor and researcher by trade, I naturally turned to books, journals, and even the web for information. I poured over statistics, medical prognoses, and firsthand accounts. I read research papers hypothesizing causes and others prophesizing outcomes. I wanted access to everything I didn't know: facts, statistics, probabilities, and outcomes. I knew my son, but I realized I was trying to understand the future.

I learned, of course, that even if I slept little and spent all my waking hours parenting and researching, knowing the future was out of reach. Instead, I focused on what I could accomplish. I focused on what I could learn to help my son right now and what I could do to make life better and our family the happiest we could be.

In this chapter, I want to hand you an action map for locating resources. Your course will likely be different than mine, but knowledge empowers. There is enough information and accumulated experience from those who have come before you to help temper the sense of loneliness that often accompanies an Asperger's diagnosis.

I recommend taking the following steps:

Find a Good Psychiatrist

You will want to find the best child psychiatrist in your area who specializes or is well versed in the treatment of autism and Asperger's syndrome. Dr. Daniels became a cornerstone in our lives. He listened to, was patient with, showed compassion for, and offered sage advice to Michael and to me. Dr. Daniels was the one who officially diagnosed Michael when he was four years old, but at that time his practice was full. We spent more than a year on a waiting list before a spot became available. I will never forget the day my husband called me to tell me we had gotten in. I felt as though we had won the Asperger's lottery. At that time, I was slowly becoming versed in the kinds of small joys I had never anticipated. Who knew that being accepted into a psychiatry practice could be grounds for such sincere celebration?

We saw Dr. Daniels every three months from when Michael was five and a half until he finished college at age twenty-two. Dr. Daniels was someone Michael listened to. He was there with us in the trenches to advise us on the myriad life challenges that steadily arose throughout Michael's youth. He gave me a constant sense of much needed relief, and for Michael he was a pillar and a sounding board.

It was not easy to wait for Dr. Daniels, but our instincts told us we should. There were few other choices, and Dr. Daniels was the standout expert in this area. We continued to see Dr. Longwood in the interim. That same instinct served as my guide through a multitude of choices and various crossroads. Yours will, too. Listen to it. When you feel in above your head, give yourself the time to listen to your gut regarding what is best. You will lose some battles, but you will win more of them.

Learn About National and Regional Organizations

Organizations like The Asperger's/Autism Network (AANE), Autism Speaks, and Autism NOW all provide critical information and resources for children and adults with ASD and their families. Autism Speaks, for example has a kit called the 100 Day Kit for Newly Diagnosed Families. It is a free downloadable or printable resource that offers a one-hundred-day roadmap for anyone recently diagnosed. The good news is that once you begin finding these resources, each one will lead you to the next. Soon you will find yourself surrounded by useful information and supportive voices.

Find Your Local Organizations

Asperger's syndrome, like many other labels that carry a stigma, has a broader community than you realized before now. Finding your way into that community will be a key to finding and growing your support system. This community looks different in every place. The local Special Education Parent Advisory Council (SEPAC) associated with your school system is a fabulous resource and is a connector for parents with children on the spectrum. Find out how to join. Ask about other local resources, support groups, and point people; they will be your guides.

It's very possible that your child's psychiatrist will be able to recommend an access point. I am fortunate enough to live in the Fairfield, Connecticut, area, which has numerous Asperger's and autism organizations, as well as other support services like social groups, OT specialists, social coaches, and reading specialists. Not everyone will have so many options. Whatever resources you have access to, find them and use them.

Local organizations will come in different forms, with different levels of utility. The main organization whose events I participated in was a Yahoo group for parents in my city. There might be a similar group in your area, a locally run group of parents with children on the spectrum who meet regularly for support and solidarity. You might also find playgroups that will offer your child the opportunity to play with other kids while you trade concerns and solutions with other parents. For older children and adults, there are also social groups for regular structured socializing. Perhaps your city or town has a local advocacy group that lobbies the schools. There also might be religious groups in your area raising awareness or offering support and guidance. I learned that my community offered a big brother/big sister mentoring program for kids up to the age of fifteen. Unfortunately, I discovered this resource too late for Michael, but this goes to show how many resources may be hidden in your community. It is crucial to seek them out.

When I first began looking into Asperger's support groups, I was struck by how different everyone's experience was. I had heard the famous quote by Dr. Stephen Shore, "If you've met one person with autism, you've met one person with autism," but I hadn't fully absorbed its reality. One of the unusual things about autism is the originality of each person's differences. No two worlds are alike. When you listen to other parents' stories and hear about their breakthroughs and realizations, you will gain more and more tools to navigate your own specific unknowns.

Educate Yourself on Available Public Resources

Your local government has likely known about Asperger's for longer than you have. There have been many public movements to improve ASD research, care, and awareness in the United States, including the Combating Autism Reauthorization Act of 2011. These movements have created legislation that provides rights and resources for your child. Each state is different, but I encourage you to familiarize yourself with local and federal laws.

At the end of this book there is a list of additional resources, such as the website for the Early Childhood Technical Assistance Center (ECTA). ECTA can provide you with resources like a free evaluation to determine if your child is qualified for government-funded intervention services. Understanding the public resources available to you can help to mitigate the financial burden of intervention as well as ensure the best care for your child.

Arm Yourself with Literature

In my opinion, knowledge, perspective, and empathy are three of the key tools to a happy life. Nothing provides access to these better than a book. People have come out *en masse* to share research, tell their personal stories, and offer guidance. Let these books speak to you and teach you. Find the one that speaks the loudest and keep it with you. For me, that book was Tony Attwood's *Asperger's Syndrome: A Guide for Parents and Professionals*.

All of Attwood's books are phenomenal, but this was my top pick. It often traveled with me in my oversized handbag so I could read and reread it at any odd moment, whether I was waiting in line at school for pickup or had arrived early to a meeting. It served as a reminder that I was never alone, regardless of how I felt in a given situation. In fact, I had extra copies of the book in my office to give to individuals involved with Michael including the school aide, sitters, and school administrators. It has never ceased to shock me how undereducated even specialists sometimes proved to be. Perhaps this kind of knowledge sharing was my first step on a longer road toward Asperger's activism and awareness raising.

Memoirs and other firsthand guides like this book are useful as well. They are just a small piece of the untapped knowledge that accumulates through personal experience.

In my research for this book, I learned a tremendous amount. My interviews with other parents as well as teachers and administrators about the diversity of challenges that come with Asperger's gave me a glimpse into the vastness of the knowledge that is out there.

Find Your Child's Champions and Show Them Gratitude

As useful as books, support groups, and research papers are, I have found that the people who most value my child are the single greatest available resource. These champions come in every form. They may come in expected roles, such as the (professional) advocate I worked with or the aide hired by the school. They may also appear casually and without warning, like a teacher who happens to see the ability or spark in your child. Perhaps you find your champions in a babysitter or a computer teacher or even a staff member at a local café who welcomes your child. Wherever they are, acknowledge them, encourage the relationships, and show your gratitude.

The first real champion of Michael's that I noticed, aside from Dr. Daniels, was his nursery school teacher, Lisa. Right away, she knew there was something special about Michael. She did not see his differences as a barrier; she saw him as a complete person worthy of praise, love, and opportunity. Middle school brought us another champion. This time it was the school guidance counselor, Christine. Christine's door wasn't open only to Michael. She was simply the kind of educator who cared deeply for each of her students. Asperger's, neurotypical, depressed, substance-dependent—it didn't matter; Christine was there with active ears, an open mind, and a huge smile.

It was Christine who, when I mentioned Michael was struggling with loneliness during lunch, started a "lunch bunch" program. The program was open to all students who once a week simply wanted to sit somewhere with an environment different than the cafeteria, with all its social matrixes. As someone who struggled to socialize or make friends, this was an enormous benefit for Michael. While such initiatives might seem small, their impact is anything but.

Unfortunately, it is not your average person who will see beyond your child's differences and straight to whom your child is. These people, the ones who do see, are like little beams of sunlight. I watched Michael's life being lit by them. I watched him bend and shape with their nourishment. There are trained professionals out there who cannot see past the barriers. There are principals, teachers, professors, lawyers, and those from disability services who never see the possibilities. They are doing their jobs, and they are doing them the ways they see fit. I watched these people look straight past my son. I witnessed his invisibility.

The years after Michael's Asperger's diagnosis still feel largely like a blur. If I had understood then how crucial relationships would be in the years to come, I would have focused more acutely on developing them early. One thing I was not good at was asking for help. I wish I had been able to set aside my own adjustment to Asperger's more quickly in order to pick up the phone and call my friends and family to tell them I needed help. The truth was that I was overwhelmed and did not want to burden anyone. Because so few people had reached out to offer help, I was convinced that few people cared.

Had I had the courage to reach out, I would have told them that Michael would struggle socially and would need friends. I would have worked with them to communicate best practices for maximizing their communication with Michael. I would have asked my siblings to accept their new nephew and to raise their children to accept their cousin. I would have done all of these things tenfold if I had been better prepared for the chance that the people I loved might say, "Not today."

If there is one thing I can't emphasize enough, it is the importance of building a support system for yourself and helping your child build one as well. You will survive on your own, but you will thrive with guidance, love, and support from those around you. Build a network that will grow and evolve as your child does.

Chapter 3
Parenting and Asperger's

Adjusting Expectations

I had a lot of plans and dreams. Who doesn't? In my mind, Michael was going to attend an independent school. He would be popular and athletic. Perhaps he would join the speech and debate club or the ski team. He might become a professor like me or follow his father's lead and become a doctor. He would be healthy, charming, and well-liked and respected by his peers and teachers. These were the thoughts I had as a brand-new mother with my first child. That is what parents do: They dream. They dream and plan, and then they learn to adjust their expectations.

Few children are exactly what their parents were expecting. Few parents, however, go through the same kind of adjustment period as the parents of a child or children on the spectrum. The shock is a big one, and the ripple effects are significant and lasting. The first lesson in parenting a child with Asperger's is learning how to adjust your expectations realistically. Adjusting your expectations, however, is different than lowering them. In this chapter I will explore some of the lessons I learned specifically regarding parenting and family life when raising a child on the spectrum.

Asperger's brought us many novel challenges. Among them were Michael's proprioception difficulties. For example, it took him many years to learn how to tie his shoes. Learning to ride a bike seemed like a distant dream for quite some time. I am still grateful for the invention of Velcro, which gave my child shoes he could manage easily on his own. I'm also grateful for the incredible, if pricy, occupational therapy (OT) place a couple of towns over from us. Learning how to ride a bike is a rite of passage that many people take for granted. We paid hundreds of dollars for Michael to learn that skill, but every penny was worth the breakthrough. OT can work wonders. Having a trained professional guide Michael in how to manage his muscles and coordination was a gift for all of us.

Michael's proprioception struggles made it difficult for him to walk down a crowded street or through a crowded hallway without bumping into people. This is a challenge, especially in North America, where people have very specific ideas of their own personal space bubbles. It always amazed me how upset people got when Michael accidentally bumped into them. It was as though people assumed he was doing it intentionally.

When Michael was living in New York, this difficulty of his terrified me. It had been bad enough in the high school hallways, but now I was scared he would be bumping into perfect strangers on the streets of New York City. What if he bumped into the wrong person at the wrong time? I lay awake at night imagining phone calls from the New York City police to inform me that my son had been beaten up for invading someone's personal space.

I never expected that as a parent I would rejoice over my son finally learning to ride a bike later than his peers or the good news that as a college student he was doing a great job of not bumping into, literally, too many people on the street. I learned to adjust my reasons for joy and celebration in parenting.

New Responses to New Behaviors

Much of what we learn about parenting comes from social modeling. We watch our parents parent us. We watch our friends' parents parent them. We watch the fictional parents on television and in movies parent their fictional children. Most of the parental role models we get, however, parent neurotypical children. At some point after Michael's diagnosis, I became acutely aware that I had no role model for how to parent him.

Michael, like most children on the spectrum, has high sensory sensitivity. For example, as a child he would not wear clothes with tags in them. I handled Michael's sensory issues in much the same way that I handled his picky taste in food. I let it go. I did not push him, at least not very hard, when it came to trying new foods and diversifying his wardrobe. I wanted him to be comfortable and look presentable.

Parenting this kid was tiring. I didn't have the energy to force him to eat everything on his plate.

Control over food and clothing was not all I had to let go of. I also had to let go of discipline to a certain extent. When Michael acted out of line, punishing simply didn't help, especially when we were in public. If he had a meltdown, it was usually easier to give in somewhat or to calm him down rather than stand my own ground. Standing my ground was risky in public, as he could resist me, and get more upset. If I put him in a time-out, he simply left it. His ADHD, especially his impulsivity, made it hard to manage him. Have you ever seen parents out with their kids and it seems like their children were trained in a military fashion, with the parent as the commander and in complete control? Well, I was never that parent.

Michael's autism altered my entire parenting style. Perhaps it simply gave me a bit of perspective. I tried not to sweat the stuff I couldn't fix. Of course, parenting a child with Asperger's and parenting a neurotypical child are different, so parenting became further complicated when Michael's little sister, Emily, came along.

ASD and Neurotypical Sibling Dynamics

My daughter, Emily, is very observant. As a younger sibling, she learned from watching her older brother and by studying his interactions with us. She became a keen observer of what Michael could get away with. If he threw a tantrum, for example, sometimes it was easiest to just give in because of his rigidity and persistence. If Emily whined, on the other hand, my instinct was to reprimand her and discourage the behavior. All siblings struggle with ideas of justice and fairness, but when one sibling is on the autism spectrum, this is only magnified.

I eventually realized that I had to be a different but equal parent to each of my children. Parenting Michael took up a huge amount of my time, which left my daughter hurt and resentful. We decided to turn to psychotherapy to identify preventative solutions to this dynamic. Therapy was enormously helpful. In light of how much time I had to spend on Michael's Asperger's-specific issues, my daughter's therapist recommended that we spend specific one-on-one time together that could feel special. This one-on-one time changed our relationship. I largely credit this to healing any possible rifts that had begun to come between us.

A year ago, I attended an autism conference at Harvard and asked the panelists about the impact of a child with Asperger's on their neurotypical siblings. The panelists agreed that not enough research has been done in this area. And so the parental groundbreaking continues for those of us facing these challenges.

Marriage and Parenting with Asperger's

My relationship with my daughter wasn't the only one that suffered from juggling the challenges of parenting a child on the spectrum. Having a child with autism is incredibly difficult on couples as well. My husband and I struggled routinely as we tried to make joint decisions and see eye to eye when it came to the best way to raise Michael. The truth was, we often didn't agree. To say parenting put a rift between my husband and me would be putting it mildly.

When Michael was in college, things felt strained to the point that I worried they might break. It is hard to be a united couple when there are unexpected stressors and the need to help one's child becomes paramount. At the end of the day, it was so often about feelings and resources. We all needed each other's time, and no one had enough to go around. Like self-care, finding a way to focus on your relationship with your spouse is crucial. You will each have your own version of parenting; sometimes it will look like wonderful teamwork, and sometimes not so much. Finding ways to keep the channels of communication open with your spouse, both in good times and in bad, will be critical.

The Parental Title

As I wore many different hats—advocate, social coach, mother, etc.—while raising Michael, one question often arose for me: How should parents of kids with Asperger's introduce themselves to their children's schools or other institutions in which their kids are involved? In elementary school and middle school, parents of children on the spectrum are expected to be part of their children's education. This is mostly true in high school as well. In college, however, this is not the case. Because the child is legally an adult, professors will oftentimes not even agree to speak with a parent.

There are helicopter parents out there—parents who hover and micromanage and refuse to give their children the autonomy they need to be independent and self-advocate.

These are not the parents we strive to be. Parents of children with autism are not helicopter parents; we are something different.

Parents of students on the spectrum need a new name. "Helicopter parent" is too derogatory. The role we play when we call a school to intervene on our children's behalf is different. We do not want to hover or micromanage. We serve an important role as part of the "team." We are adults playing a critical role in these young persons' development, and the people on the other end of the phone or across the desk or on the receiving end of an email communication should appreciate that. We are the "involved parents," the "caring parents," or the "team parents."

Parents of kids on the spectrum want things to go smoothly but often have to be involved to make that happen. The last thing they need is to deal with accusations of being overinvolved. If you have a college-age child who is on the spectrum, having him or her sign forms with the college's office of disability services will make it possible for that office to speak to you. This is critical for the success of the student. In this way, parents can still be part of the "team," however official or unofficial it is.

My continuing role as a highly involved parent was not something I aspired to. I learned to play the role out of necessity; I found little sense of joy in the ongoing advocacy and troubleshooting. However, I don't have any regrets about my involvement.

Once things go bad for your child—when there is bullying, depression, and misunderstanding—there is little choice but to be involved. In that instance, trust of the system is replaced by the tiger mom quality that comes with the instinctive need to protect one's child. Until school systems start doing their part to support these kids, parents need to pick up the slack and advocate to get students what they need. I'm sorry that I had to replace parts of my life that could have been more enjoyable with ongoing advocacy and support for my son. Some days I even resent it. But, given the miracle of what my son has become—his sense of maturity, independence, and self-confidence—I do not regret it. I did what I had to do, and I'm grateful that things have turned out the way they have.

Learning What Works

The most critical thing I have learned in parenting is to trust what works. There are a million opinions out there about best practices, and some of them are incredibly useful and good advice. Others, though, will not work. It can be hard not to question yourself and your own abilities as a parent when a critically acclaimed best practice seems to belly flop in your household. Don't sweat it. Trust your own judgment as a parent and learn the tricks that work for you.

In the school system, for example, you will find that there are "helpers" and "hurters." Helpers are the potential mentors, aids, confidants, friends, and other people who care. They are the "yes" people, the special ones who find a way to say, "Yes. Let's make this happen." Hurters are the bureaucrats, teachers, and administrators who fail to embrace your child or, at the extreme, find a way not to deal with your child at all or to bully or put your child in harm's way. They are the "no" people. Trust your gut. You will quickly figure out whom you can trust, whom you should avoid, whom to stand up to, whom to value, and whom to doubt.

You should also trust your gut on little things. If something works, do it again. Learn the tricks of success for your child. Some will be big, and some will be small, but even small actions' impact can be large. One of my little tricks was something I used every time we traveled on an airplane. For Michael, being in an enclosed space for a long period of time was particularly challenging. I found that if I packed new games or toys to give Michael on the flight, I could usually distract him long enough to prevent any major breakdowns.

When Michael was little, it didn't occur to me that this wasn't something every parent had to do when they traveled. It was like a little ritual. The day before a flight or sometimes the day of, I would run to the store to buy a travel toy. I avoided anything too expensive or breakable. I tried to find things that were compact but engaging and that would not disturb other passengers. This was something that worked for me. My son brimmed with excitement knowing he had to wait until the plane took off to open his backpack and discover whatever surprise awaited him.

Finding what works as a parent isn't always easy. Sometimes you discover it through trial and error. Other times you listen to the advice of others. Sometimes you don't find a great solution. But when we do, like discovering the trick of a travel toy, it feels like winning the lottery. When we don't find it, it can feel awful. If part of parenting is about learning what works, then the flip side of it is learning to let go of what you can't control. It's impossible to find a solution to everything, and that's okay. Learn what works. Let go of the pieces you can't control.

The Superpower of Parenthood

Some of my most inspired moments are when I meet other parents of children on the spectrum. More specifically, it's when I meet other mothers—or, as I like to call them, the heroes of autism. Recently, I was staying at the hotel where Michael and I used to stay when I visited him in college. On this particular weekend, a year and a half after Michael moved to San Francisco, I was sitting in the restaurant bar when I noticed a mother and her son. The son had his face buried in his phone, did not make eye contact, and engaged with the mother infrequently. I felt an immediate pang of recognition and empathy.

I struck up a conversation with this mother. She told me that her son was on the spectrum, and I told her about Michael. It turned out that they were from Michigan and had just been on vacation in Florida at Disney World. When it was time to go home, however, her son had refused to get on the plane to go back to Michigan. He struggled with flying, and when he refused to board the plane, it was nearly impossible to get him to change his mind. So, this mother had decided to rent a car in Orlando while her husband flew home with their other kids. Instead of driving directly to Michigan, she drove her son to New York along the way so that they could go to the Nintendo store, a favorite of her son's. From

New York, she decided that she would reassess how her son was doing and make plans to get home from there.

I stared at this woman who had just driven alone at the drop of a hat from Florida to New York *en route* to Michigan out of devotion for her son and with an understanding of the challenges he faced and a determination to make his life more comfortable. I was impressed that her husband had been so supportive of the decision and had encouraged her to go. I was also impressed at how quickly both of them had been able to change gears and regroup. I also complimented her hair because it looked as though she had taken the time to treat herself to a salon appointment.

I felt as though there should be a superhero action figure named after this woman. *Wonder Mom*: the woman who drives for double-digit hours on the spur of the moment out of unconditional love for her son (and because ultimately it was the only option). She made it seem like nothing as she told me the story, which is when I decided that I believed in a kind of superpower—the magical ability parents have to do extraordinary things for the sake of their ASD children.

She is definitely one of the heroes of autism. I found myself thinking that there should be some sort of hall of fame, some recognition for these heroes, to replace the silence that currently surrounds them. The next chapter of this book is dedicated to all the women (and men) spending their lives doing what she's doing.

Chapter 4
The Parent as Superhero/Case Manager

Throughout my research for this book—including interviews with parents, teachers, and school administrators, among others—one theme consistently rose to the top: the power of perseverance. The children whose parents worked day by day and issue by issue and never gave up were the children most likely to reach their potential. The parents of these children are the ones who truly embrace their roles as case managers.

It is safe to say that before we begin most jobs, we apply for them and are accepted. There are exceptions, of course, but this is a path with which we are all familiar. Even parenthood, a job not explicitly clear in its demands, usually gives us roughly nine months to prepare for what lies ahead. Becoming the case manager for my son's life with Asperger's was a job I'd neither applied for nor realized I'd begun.

The reality is that managing Asperger's in today's world, a task that goes above and beyond parenting, is a full-time job. It is a job that you probably don't have much experience with and one you didn't sign up for. Your ASD child's development, however, will continue to evolve whether you step up to the challenge of steering the ship or not. This responsibility sneaks up on you because at first glance it feels like someone else must certainly be in charge. What do you know about Asperger's, anyway?

Initially, as I've said, I looked to our pediatrician for leadership, followed by Michael's psychiatrist, Dr. Daniels. These doctors were critical resources for our understanding of our son's behavior and development. Suddenly, however, there was school to think about. Who was supposed to help me there? And what about playdates? Where was the magic wand of justice that would allow my child to socialize like other children? Who would be there to explain to other parents why my son behaved the way he did? Who could instill in all the other children the gift of acceptance? And what impact would Michael's Asperger's have on his sister?

Those were the more abstract challenges. We also had the mundane to think about. What about trips to the barber? To the grocery store? To restaurants? What about flying? Taxi rides? Public restrooms? Sports teams? School lunch? Recess? Riding the bus? What about school interviews? Job interviews? Standardized tests? How would we find an understanding and competent babysitter? Could Michael go to summer camp? Take music lessons? Participate in after-school activities? I have learned that this list never stops. It is what makes up every single aspect of your child's life. I have also learned, and you will too if you haven't already, that there is absolutely no one in charge of managing the breadth of these challenges other than you and your partner.

So what does that mean? It means *you* are the case manager; you are in charge of your child's development.

In this chapter, I will guide you through the numerous ways that parents can become case managers for their children with Asperger's and what exactly it entails. Every parent, depending on his or her own professional and personal workload, will react differently to having this set of tasks thrust upon him or her. Some will be better at delegating within their support systems; others will learn the art of juggling, making and following to-do lists, and sifting through the plethora of daily challenges to ensure the priorities rise to the top and are addressed accordingly.

Have you ever experienced that moment at the doctor's office when the doctor suggests a solution to a problem, but you know that this solution either results in another problem or is too difficult to implement? If you have a really good doctor, he or she might realize this and say something like, "What we need to do here is take a more holistic approach." This realization is now your job.

It is a critical moment, one in which we understand the futility of reacting to problems as they arise—as if in a vacuum—instead of constantly monitoring the complete picture to comprehend cause and effect. It is this holistic approach that we need to take with any parenting but especially when parenting a child with Asperger's.

Here are my top ten tips for being a successful holistic case manager.

1. Advocate

If something doesn't feel right with your child's development, speak up. Ask for something. You might not even know what exactly you are asking for, but asking for help is often the only way to get it.

"The system" is that giant, all-encompassing, living, breathing thing that includes education, health care, extracurricular activities, and the professional world. The education system is like a single pie, and there are never enough slices to go around. The only way to get a piece of that pie is to ask for it. Ask for it and then advocate if it doesn't arrive. Every player in the system has different goals for the finite resources available. Your child has no spokesperson other than you to advocate for those resources.

The fewer resources a school spends on your child, the more it can spend elsewhere. For you, the more resources your child has, the brighter his or her future will be. These two perspectives do not necessarily come together harmoniously. The resources you might request will come in all shapes and forms, likely including but not limited to an Individualized Educational Plan (IEP), reading support, speech and language therapy, occupational therapy (OT), schoolwork modification, aides, applied behavior analysis (ABA), and standardized testing accommodations.

Simply familiarizing yourself with the resources available can be a steep learning curve. The school will likely not open its drawers to show you every resource in there; you will have to do research to learn what is available. You will have to speak up when something is not right and continue speaking up until the problem has been solved. Speaking up to the school system will mean putting requests in writing. If you want to get a response or be taken seriously, sending an email, registered letter, or fax is critical. Express what you mean verbally and then back it up with a request in writing. That way you will be more likely to receive your child's share of available resources.

In a perfect world, every parent whose child is on the spectrum would be an advocate for another. Unfortunately, that is often not how things are. The single-pie system does not breed unity. Far too often the reality is that the resources your neighbor is receiving would dwindle if you requested the same ones. This can create tension and a sense of secrecy within the community of parents who have children with Asperger's.

Finding a way to rise above this war for resources is a challenge. I believe the more unity there is between parents, the more powerful the asking voice can be. Seeking out parents who have been through similar circumstances is key; they are more open and able to help. Join the local Special Education Parent Advisory Council (SEPAC) that advises the school district. The Individuals with Disabilities Education Act (IDEA) requires each state to establish and maintain an advisory panel for the purpose of guiding the state special education staff in the education of eligible children with disabilities. By law, all school districts should have SEPACs.

You can also receive legal training to enhance your advocacy skills. I didn't know about the role of parent advocate until recently when I began an advocacy course through the Parent Council Training Institute (PCTI), which is part of the Federation for Children with Special Needs. I met informed parents who knew the nuances of IEPs, 504s (Section 504 of the Rehabilitation Act of 1973), placements, and other topics (see Chapter 6 for more information on IEPs and 504s). Learning how to access the law has been empowering. I highly recommend taking this course. As a case manager, you need to ensure your child is receiving the best available resources at all times. This, as is probably evident by now, often means ongoing education and advocating on your child's behalf.

Whether one conflict ends in success or defeat, there will always be a next fight, and each one needs an energy source. These battles don't line up neatly one after the other; they sprout randomly and without warning. Sometimes they don't even arrive chronologically; rather, they sneak up from the past or happen without notice in the present, or while looking toward the still hazy future. If there is one certainty that I can promise you through this whole adventure, it's that your to-do list will never want for causes worth fighting for, which leads me to my next point.

2. Prioritize (The Art of Task-Management)

Successful advocacy, activism, persuasion, and lobbying all share a common requirement: organization. Being a case manager means first being a manager. To manage a task load to achieve your desired results, you must be conscious of every task and where it falls in order of priority. These priorities change constantly, impacted by the daily or weekly influx of new and unexpected tasks. I recommend that you keep an actual physical list and consider ranking the tasks in order of importance. This will not only help keep you organized and prevent things from slipping through the cracks, but it will also relieve you of the mental load of carrying this information around in your brain all the time.

When I talk about things slipping through the cracks, I'm not talking about small things. Without guidance, our brains react to crises as they occur. Living with Asperger's in a neurotypical world means living with the potential for unpredictable crises at any moment. It is important to create a strategy for crisis management so that your response is intentional instead of reactionary. If you do not sharpen your management skills, life can feel chaotic. I believe this chaos is at times avoidable, but it takes intentional and consistent effort to achieve such a feat.

Throughout this book, I will refer to tasks and crises in a couple of ways: issues that are "in the weeds" or "in the trenches" and the big-picture issues. The latter, ongoing long-term issues are tremendously important and can often be overshadowed by the weeds. It is not easy to maintain two perspectives at once, but it is critical to your child's development. Every weed is somehow connected to the long haul. Understanding that relationship, even if this reflection happens after the fact, will be very useful in making the best long-term choices for your child.

What does it look like in the trenches? Well, it depends on the day. In elementary school we often found ourselves in the trenches over seemingly small but important social problems. In fifth grade, for example, one of Michael's main disappointments was that he was rarely invited to birthday parties. Even when the other kids were included, Michael was often left off the list. This wasn't intentional cruelty on the part of other parents or kids; Michael didn't have many friends and the other kids didn't particularly enjoy spending time with him. But this knowledge didn't lessen Michael's feelings of hurt and confusion when another day of school brought stories of another party he hadn't been invited to. That year, we were lucky that Michael had an incredible teacher. She announced to his class that it was mandatory for students to invite everyone (or at least all the girls or all the boys) in the class if they were going to have a party. This definitely improved Michael's quality of life.

Meanwhile, we were managing other long-term issues. Michael's ADD/ADHD caused him many challenges at school and at home. We knew it would continue to be a challenge for him throughout childhood and into adulthood. We worked regularly with his doctors to manage his medications and alternative therapies in order to work toward the most successful outcome for Michael. Many of the short-term issues we faced correlated directly to a problem with a strategy for one of the long-term issues. Finding a way to connect and analyze these correlations was critical for Michael's long-term happiness.

I had by no means mastered these ideas when I first started this case management job. There is so much I wish I could do over again. If I'd understood, for example, the critical importance of speech and language therapy at a young age, I would have focused much harder on finding Michael the resources he needed and ensuring that his developmental barriers were addressed to the largest extent possible.

Looking back, I have to admit that speech and language therapy fell through the cracks. At the time, I didn't really realize my son had a speech issue. Kids often sound kind of goofy, and it is hard to listen for a dropped *r* or look at the place one puts the tongue to form the sounds of letters if you haven't been trained. Michael still has a lisp today, one I believe would be gone if I had known how and where to focus my energies as a young mom. Don't let things like speech get lost when you're buried in the weeds. Seemingly non-urgent issues can still be time sensitive.

The good news is that being a successful task manager helps you be proactive rather than reactive. While you cannot know exactly what you need to do in advance, being organized helps you channel your energy (which often stems from concern, frustration, confusion, and anger) toward the items on your to-do list for your child. Hopefully, being proactive will help you feel more in control as you try to manage the issues surrounding autism.

Take time to celebrate big and small successes and achievements. I remember the day my son rode a two-wheel bicycle for the first time with help of his OT instructor. My husband and I celebrated that night by watching him ride his bike at home. The achievement felt so large; it was a rite of passage, much like passing the driver's test, graduating from high school, completing his bar mitzvah, and graduating from college. We celebrated each success, big and small, along the way. This was critical to the "work hard, play hard" approach.

3. Be a Social Coach

In your first several months (and years) of parenting a child with Asperger's, you will learn a tremendous amount. It will likely equate to earning an advanced degree on the subject, and this will be compounded by visceral day-to-day experiences. In essence, you find that in very short order you become an expert in a subject you likely knew very little about. Most people you will interact with on a regular basis, however, are like the old you. They don't have a clue. You have to become a guide. The notion of social coaching is twofold: you must be a social coach for your child and for the people with whom your child interacts.

When Michael was young, I often relied on Carol Gray's idea of "social stories" to find a mutual understanding between Michael and my different social perspectives.[3] This was useful for grasping complex ideas as well as mundane ones, like going out for ice cream—something that might seem simple for a neurotypical child. When Michael and I went out for ice cream, we first created a social story. This story, a combination of words and even images, previewed the stages of events for Michael: First, we would get out of the car. Then we would enter the ice cream shop. After that, we would wait in line behind the people who were already there. We would each select an ice cream flavor and tell our choices to the person working behind the counter. When our turn came, we would pay for the ice cream. Then we would sit in a seat by the window to eat the ice cream. After that, we would leave the shop and get back into the car to go home.

---

[3] "Social Stories," Carol Gray Social Stories, accessed 01/08/17, http://carolgraysocialstories.com/social-stories/.

Without the social story ahead of the actual trip to the ice cream shop, chaos could easily ensue. Instead of waiting in line, Michael would want to cut in front of everyone and sprawl across the counter where people were trying to pay. Or he might run around the store, trying out different seats and I would have to chase him around and try to physically lift him from wherever he placed himself. With the social stories, however, Michael understood what to expect. If he started to cut in line, I would remind him of the part of the story where we were supposed to wait; he would understand and get back in line.

The other side of social coaching—the one that involves educating others on the best ways to interact with Michael— arose frequently with extended family, parents, and babysitters, as well as teachers and school administrators. Because not all adults in the school system are trained in autism, the job falls to you to explain your child's behavior. But that's not all; you will also need to explain to teachers and administrators what they can do to relieve the challenge of communicating with your child. I've learned that educating or coaching teachers and administrators is filled with nuances. Adults must be open and willing to learn, which often means you must strategize ways for your knowledge to be heard by others.

4. Encourage

This tip applies to neurotypical and Asperger's kids alike. Every child deserves support and encouragement when it comes to activities in which they show interest and skill.

With a child on the spectrum, however, it isn't always easy to encourage those interests, as they can differ from the usual sports or theater program. Additionally, kids with autism usually struggle with perseveration. This can materialize through repetitive thoughts, ideas, and speech, as well as a constantly changing obsession or special interest. Perseveration is not something to let go unchecked, but it is also not something that should be suppressed or punished.

Ask yourself: How can I find a good balance between interest and over-focus? How can I help my child's struggle with rigidity or resistance to change? How can I help my child identify his or her skills and hone them?

Michael zeroed in on his interests so acutely and cycled through them so routinely that a friend of mine ended up making us a painting to illustrate the different phases of Michael's childhood. The painting was a simple list in clean white letters on a black backdrop, paying tribute to the beauty and challenge of perseveration. It included items like Brio egg pull toy, easel painting, making Silly Putty, Mariah Carey, Martin Luther King Jr., and taping award shows. There was no rhyme or reason that connected Michael's obsessions or helped us predict what would come next. We allowed him to move naturally through his own shifting interests. Some experts suggest limiting time spent on special interests so they don't interfere with other aspects of life, but new voices suggest that these interests should be monitored but encouraged. Finding the right balance can be difficult. In Michael's case, John and I decided that being cautiously encouraging was more important and valuable than punishing or discouraging.

When it came to honing Michael's skills and abilities, we felt the same way, but it wasn't always as easy to figure out what to encourage. In middle school, we were grateful for the insight of Michael's guidance counselor, Christine. It was Christine who, when I shared with her that Michael had too much time on his hands because he had neither friends nor after-school activities, suggested he try tutoring. Michael was a very gifted student. Why not see if he could help other students improve? Michael was excited by the idea, and it ended up being a great success. In fact, Michael became such a popular tutor in middle school that kids requested his help left and right. In high school, he continued to practice this skill as a paid private tutor. We used to joke that around exam time and especially before chemistry tests he suddenly became the most popular kid at school.

Developing a skill is a game changer. Tutoring raised Michael's self-esteem and provided him with transferable skills that we will discuss more in Chapter 8: Autism in the Professional World. The main lesson I learned with Michael is that encouragement beats discouragement without fail, and sometimes it takes being open to your child's interests, even when you would prefer to discuss something, *anything*, else. Tutoring for Michael was like being on the basketball team or participating in a school play; it was social and equally rewarding.

5. Sharpen Your "Aspergerism" Radar

Kids with disabilities can face a lifetime of stereotyping, discrimination, and harassment, just like kids living with the other -*isms* out there: racism, anti-Semitism, sexism, etc. I began calling the discrimination Michael faced *Aspergerism*. It probably seems like it should be easy to tell when your child is being discriminated against, but it's not as straightforward as it seems.

The problem with Aspergerism, like most other forms of discrimination, is that those perpetrating the discrimination often don't realize they are doing it. In addition, they often don't know what the disability is, as Asperger's is typically an invisible disability. And worse, they are frequently the most adamant deniers that such a form of discrimination exists. Aspergerism can manifest in several different ways. It may arise in relation to likeability. This tends to show itself through bullying and social neglect. Aspergerism can also arise from fear. In Michael's experience, this resulted in labeling, restricted privileges, and (unnecessary) police intervention.

While raising Michael, I had to hone my Aspergerism detection skills so I could identify when he was being discriminated against in order to work to prevent future discrimination. It is a long, bumpy road, and for those of us who don't have previous personal experience interacting with people with disabilities, it will likely include a good, long inward look to identify any tendencies we ourselves have toward this -*ism* so that we can both overcome it and identify it in others.

6. Attend the Meetings

This is potentially one of the most tedious, unexciting pieces of advice I will offer. Support groups, community groups, school meetings, and other social, professional, or religious events pertaining to Asperger's will probably not be the highlight of your day. They can be long, boring, unpleasant, unhelpful, and even scary or upsetting. Every now and then, however, you'll get a little *aha* moment when a bell will go off and suddenly you understand your child better than you did before. Or you'll meet someone who introduces you to a resource you didn't know was available. Or another parent will discuss a nightmare scenario that you probably would have headed straight into if you hadn't heard his or her story on that particular day.

You can't know which meetings will be pointless and which will bring a mild breakthrough. I believe the breakthroughs make it worth sitting through all (or at least most of) the rest. Find whatever patience you can and make yourself show up. Remember, the value isn't just in the meetings themselves; many worthwhile interactions take place informally over a coffee break conversation or during a chance meeting while walking to your car. These can be the life-altering interactions that make all the meetings worth it.

Be intentional and selective about the meetings you attend. With support groups, for example, it's a matter of finding a good fit. Some of the support groups and other parent groups I attended when Michael was younger felt like gripe sessions that weren't useful to me. I'm sure other parents out there found that the exact same groups were a perfect fit for them. Find the resource groups that are helpful for you and then show up.

It was in a Yahoo support group meeting that I met Joanne, a woman who later became a close friend and a pillar in my Asperger's support system. She offered to look at Michael's IEP, because we had been struggling with it and she had more experience on the subject. It was a lifesaver. I often found that the topics of the Yahoo support group meetings varied and some were more relevant for me than others, but meeting Joanne was worth it all.

As a case manager, you will acquire a lot of your knowledge through these meetings. Some of it may sit as latent knowledge until it is suddenly activated in a meeting with the school or with a lawyer. A little voice might play in the back of your head, reminding you that you've heard about this experience before, and you have heard about an outcome that was a success. I will say simply that, like exercise, paying taxes, or any other task that feels hard until it's over, I was usually glad that I went, even if the highlight was going home.

7. Take Care of Yourself

Here it is, my all-encompassing yet minimalist survival tidbit for you. Being a case manager is hard because it means you are often the make-or-break factor in any given situation. You are the sounding board, the rebound, and the safety net. Sometimes your child comes to you first, but he or she will always come to you as a last resort. You are your child's main support system, and as any other Asperger's parent out there can attest to, it is exhausting. It is rewarding, but it drains you in a way that is difficult to describe.

You are critical to your child's care, but let me mention the flip side of that, which is also of critical importance: self-care. We all know we can only be as strong for others as we are for ourselves. We can only give as much of ourselves as there is to give. Find the thing you need and give it to yourself, whether it's regular exercise, ice cream, manicures, kickboxing, golf, a dog, or whatever.

I have found that having my own therapist as well as taking a hard but motivating cycling class are key to my sanity and sometimes my son's as well. I know I am not alone in this. Many of my friends have also found that getting a therapist can be a crucial act of self-care. My therapist, Maria, was not only a support system for me, but she also offered her services as an objective third party when Michael needed insight as well. When Michael felt most stuck and I was at a loss for what to do next, I would say, "Let's call Maria!" and Michael would agree. And so we had a consistent, reliable, objective opinion to help us up and out of the trenches. More than helping with Michael, though, Maria helped me with me.

Self-care comes in all shapes and sizes. Do whatever you need to feel like the strongest, most capable, and most grateful person you can be. Do this for yourself.

8. Learn to Shift Gears

I had coffee with a good friend recently while doing the research for this book. She mentioned something that I had never given serious thought to before. She said to me, "I was always amazed by how willing you were to change directions." It took a minute for this notion to sink in, but when it did, I realized she was onto something. I had spent so much of my time going so fast that I didn't always notice I was going in a particular direction. I often didn't have the luxury to think about which way I was headed; I simply pointed myself at whatever task needed doing and I threw my whole self at it.

But sometimes, as my friend pointed out, two back-to-back tasks might take you in seemingly opposite directions. Such was the case with Michael's college applications. After throwing ourselves into getting Michael into his first-choice school, we had to throw ourselves equally in an opposite direction when plan A didn't work out. This ability to shift gears without despair was key to Michael's success. The next lesson, however, took me a bit longer to learn and embrace.

9. Don't Rush Worry

It was while shifting gears and restarting the college application process that I first heard this phrase. I had gone to Michael's advocate to discuss his school choices and the risk of not being accepted (more on advocates in chapter 6). I expressed my concerns to her, including the fact that he had refused to choose a backup college. I feared what Michael's future might look like if he didn't get into any of these schools.

She responded clearly and firmly: "Don't rush worry."

She went on to say that because there were so many

possible outcomes for every scenario, to try to guess and be prepared for each was impossible. Not only that, but assuming a negative outcome and spending time worrying in advance about the impact of that hypothetical difficulty was a waste of energy and created the kind of stress that worked like poison in the body. It wasn't something I'd ever thought about before, but I've thought about it over and over since.

As parents and case managers, we have plenty on our plates. Why not remove the additional stress of hypothetical disasters? After that conversation I made a promise to myself: I will, to the best of my human ability, address the challenges that exist now. I encourage you to do the same. Celebrate the joys that exist now. Do not try to worry about future problems before they have arrived. There just isn't enough energy in the world to waste it trying to solve potential future problems.

Finally, whether you've achieved the nirvana-like ability to live in the moment or not, in the next tip I present to you a final and meaningful offering to remember in your role as case manager.

10. "Never, Never, Never Give Up."

I was on vacation when I saw this Winston Churchill quote on a trinket in a little gift shop. Cliché as it may be, it struck me to my core that this had to be the tagline for my life as a case manager. There were numerous times when I was ready to throw in the towel. There were times when I wanted to curl up into a little ball and disappear. There were times when I was filled with rage or with the kind of frustration and sadness that feels physically tangible. My notions of justice and fairness changed, warped, and sometimes evaporated altogether. But then there was all the rest.

There was Michael's excitement over being the most popular tutor in high school every time exams rolled around. There was the smile on his face when he received his early decision acceptance to Ivy League school number one. There was the relief that came when he transferred to Ivy League school number two after a disastrous few semesters. And finally, like some dream rolling in from someone else's life, there was the sight of Michael walking across the stage to accept his diploma at his Ivy League university graduation. I had no idea that pride or love could swell so big or heal so many of the things that had come before.

So yes, it is worth pushing through the hard times. Sometimes you just have to take a deep breath, and decide to never give up, no matter what.

Chapter 5
Asperger's and Social Life

You know you are raising either a prodigy or a child with significant social deficits when your toddler delights in interactions with adults but is disinterested in other children. In my case, it was a little of both. Socializing did not come easily to Michael. This is common for kids with Asperger's. The entire notion of relationships is quite nuanced, and social interactions often play out on a frequency Michael simply cannot hear. When he was younger, this did not pose enormous challenges, but by middle school Michael became painfully conscious of his own social barriers. This chapter will explore some of the most personal aspects of life with Asperger's.

Social Struggle and Early Intervention

To be the best guide for Michael socially, I first needed to understand how his mind worked and what his thought process looked like. Once Michael reached middle school, he talked often and openly about wishing he had more friends. He also spoke openly about not understanding how people made friends. I tried to dig a little deeper into Michael's ideas on this subject.

When he was in sixth grade, I asked him, "Michael, what qualities are you looking for in a friend?"

"I don't know."

"What qualities are you *not* looking for in a friend?"

"I don't know," he said again.

This was so foreign to me. How was it possible that my son's brain was a *tabula rasa* when it came to relationships?

I prodded a little further. "Would you like your friends to be kind? Smart? Funny? Would you like them to have similar interests as you?"

"I guess so," Michael said.

It was as if I had been speaking another language, one that Michael wanted to understand but really couldn't piece together. It took time to learn that the whole notion of relationships—both creating and maintaining them—really was a foreign language for Michael. He went to work on learning this social language, but it took him another decade to really hone those skills.

In middle school, we realized Michael would need assistance if he wanted to close the gap between his social abilities and those of his peers. The school offered us a social coach with whom Michael met every week. Though she wasn't perfect, she did help lessen the gap. Unfortunately, we were never able to close it enough.

Michael suffered in middle school because of the contrast between his acute awareness that he was different and his very limited ability to become like his peers. He described this time as feeling like there was an unspoken agreement between all the other students that he was different and that it was okay to exclude him from all social activities because of it. Despite my best efforts, Michael was lonely and ostracized. It all felt somewhat manageable, however, until the bullying began.

Bullying

Unfortunately, being on the spectrum often leaves you incredibly vulnerable to bullies. Michael experienced many incidents of bullying in middle school, high school, and college. Perhaps it was his desperation to be liked that augmented the cruelty of his worst bullying experience.

During Michael's sophomore year in high school, there was an all-school party. Everyone in the sophomore class stayed in the school overnight. Michael felt, and his father and I agreed, that this would not be a good situation for him. Happily, Michael was invited by some of his peers to an alternative sophomore party. "The other sophomore party" was going to be more low-key with just a few people and would take place at someone's house. This was definitely something Michael could manage.

Michael was thrilled for his first real social adventure. He packed his sleepover bag, and John drove him to the boy's house and waited outside to make sure he got in okay. Michael walked up the front porch steps and knocked on the door. There was no answer. He rang the bell, and no one answered. He tried the knob. The door opened easily, but suddenly the security alarm went off and the dog leapt to attention. With the alarm and the dog's barks sounding in his ears, Michael ran back to the car. John drove him home.

It quickly became painfully clear that there had been no "other sophomore party." Michael had been the butt of an awful joke. And what if John hadn't waited? What were those kids' intentions? The police could have come and arrested Michael for breaking and entering. The dog could have attacked him. Most brutal, though, was the sharp disappointment that came with realizing that not only did he not have new friends but also the people he thought were his friends were getting some sick sense of satisfaction from his pain. By the end of high school, these kinds of horrific bullying experiences pushed Michael into a depression.

John and I did everything we could think to do: We gave unconditional love and support. We addressed the bullying with the school. We advocated for better care for our son. But nothing can undo the pain and damage caused by bullying. Michael, however, was miraculous in his own toughness. He continued to push ahead and persevere one day at a time.

As a parent, it is horrible to see your child bullied. You feel powerless, angry, and incapable. I wanted to go after every bully who hurt my son, but I knew the reciprocal impact it had on the victims of bullying. Instead, I insisted that the principals of Michael's middle school and high school take bullying seriously and take preventive action. I did the same when Michael was in college with the Office of Student Life and Disability Services. Though I did not have many specific successes to show for my efforts as a bullying lobbyist at the time, I do believe there were enough of us championing this cause to make a difference.

Connecticut now has antibullying laws, and schools have created antibullying policies and workshops to teach students what is expected. If your child is being bullied, speak up. Schools can have the largest impact to end bullying. Most importantly, ensure your child has a loving support system to come home to. So long as your child has a strong foundation, he or she will be able to survive the lowest actions of his or her peers.

Bullying is a significant problem for students across America, but kids with Asperger's definitely bear more than their fair share of it. I hope Michael's story can help you know what to watch out for so that your child can avoid wherever possible the bullying he experienced.

Coping with Depression

It's likely that the seeds of depression were born in middle school, when Michael first became aware that he was on the autism spectrum. Knowing he was different from his peers and that there wasn't much he could do to change it was a hard pill to swallow. His friendlessness, followed by severe high school and college bullying only compounded his sense of isolation.

Michael's struggle with depression in high school became acute in college. He became obese and inactive. He stopped sleeping well and stopped attending classes regularly. Michael came within inches of not graduating from college, even after years of fighting for himself. We used every resource possible, from the university health department, to my own therapist, to doctors, lawyers, and advocates to help push Michael through his darkest time.

Even after graduation, Michael felt like the future was blank for him. He hadn't been able to push himself to apply for jobs toward the end of college the way his peers had. It wasn't until he moved back home after graduation that he applied to several companies, largely thanks to the support of a friend of Michael's who truly believed in his intellect and ability.

Everything changed when Michael received a job offer from Apple. His depression lifted the way fog does when the sun finally cracks through. Positive feedback—especially external to your family—is a game changer. The job was in San Francisco and started right away. He geared up to move immediately and did so within weeks.

Sometimes San Francisco feels like the big break we'd all been waiting for, the light we'd been telling ourselves must exist at the end of the tunnel. Michael's life changed, and so did ours. He started work, and with his new role and responsibilities came a self-awareness that was somewhat foreign to him. Michael noticed his clothing, his body, and his hygiene, and he started changing his outward appearance. With this change came higher self-esteem. Michael made friends. For possibly the first time in his life, he made real friends.

Michael made friends to socialize with outside of work, he made friends in his line of work to share ideas and experiences with, and he made friends with people at the gym.

He even rekindled acquaintances from Ivy League school number two. Recent graduates he knew well (or not so well) came and stayed with him while they interviewed at Apple, and they remained friends when some of them moved to San Francisco.

As a parent and someone who had witnessed Michael's life for the entire twenty-two years before he moved to San Francisco, I was somewhat in awe. In high school and college Michael had had a bad habit of saying whatever he thought about anyone at any moment without first considering the consequences. He didn't understand that talking about one person to another was not a way to make better friendships. In fact, this was one of the traits that hindered him in making friends easily. Suddenly, in San Francisco he was more reserved and thoughtful when interacting with his friends.

I visited him about six months after he moved, and I went out for ice cream with his friends. They were great. They were kind, thoughtful, nice people. Watching Michael interact with them made my heart happy. Was this my son—well-dressed, healthy, bantering, and having thoughtful conversations with his self-made group of friends?

One person with whom he interacted in San Francisco was more like Michael used to be. Michael had hesitations about spending time with him because this guy was impulsive. He talked about other people and said out loud whatever he was thinking. When Michael told me this, I asked him what had changed for him. What made it different to make friends in San Francisco versus elsewhere?

"Well," he said, "I learned to think before I speak. That's made a big difference."

I nearly fainted. For Michael's entire life I'd been trying to coach him on this subject. I'd tried in every way I knew to work on Michael's impulsivity and his habit of speaking whatever came into his mind. Now, just like that, it had finally sunk in. In that moment, I felt like I was meeting Michael for the first time. More importantly, I finally felt at ease with his future success and happiness. I went home breathing from such a happy place. I hadn't felt that way since Michael was born.

Socialization: What Is Your Role?

One of the most difficult challenges parents of children with Asperger's face is to know when and how to insert ourselves. What role are we supposed to play in our children's social lives, that precious area that generally exists between a child and his or her friends and peers? Raising Michael, I found that I was constantly negotiating with myself over this topic. Should I step in? Should I let him fight his own battles? In the end, I found that the most important role I could play was that of his mother—a support system, a source of unconditional love, a champion, a teammate, a safety net, and a source of stability.

Leading by example was one of the best forms of social coaching I had to offer. Given that Michael lacked social instincts and struggled with the language of relationship nuance, it was crucial that he had someone to observe. Watching the social cues of others is a key way that children with Asperger's learn to act and interact. Throughout Michael's life, I have tried to be conscious of my own behavior, and when necessary, I have explained my actions and choices to him. I noticed a sense of maturation when he was in his twenties; Michael's brain filled up like a toolbox of memorized interactions. These were tools he could pull out and use at any point in his future.

Another crucial role I played as a parent was finding Michael the best possible Asperger's experts and therapists to meet with regularly. Dr. Daniels played a critical role throughout Michael's life. In college, we found Michael an additional expert; Dr. Masserman—from the best autism hospital program in the state—was very positive about Michael's future and instilled much of the hope in Michael that would get him through Ivy League school number two and into the next chapter of his life. Good therapy and family support were also pillars that helped Michael navigate his own social life and the hardships that came with it.

Michael's path through the complex world of socialization, friendship, and school life was a long and winding one. It was excruciating for him at times, especially when the bullying was most acute. It was also excruciating for John and me to watch our son experience this kind of pain. We would not wish it on anyone else's child.

It was clear that Michael's resilience and will to keep going was critical to his completion of high school and college. Even after high school, he was a self-proclaimed optimist, determined to prevent future students from having negative experiences. It's impossible to know in advance what kind of experiences your child's social life will bring. With the right support, however, your child will survive adolescence and move toward maturity and a happier, independent life.

Chapter 6
Navigating the School System

An Early Understanding of a Long Road

John and I had an unexpected meeting at my son's school in January 1997. It was a pretty little private school that reminded everyone of the little red schoolhouse. Michael was five years old.

"We don't feel," the director began, "that Michael is a good fit for our school."

My son was only in kindergarten. He had been diagnosed with Asperger's just a few months earlier, and already he was being kicked out of his first school. John and I both began speaking at the same time.

"How is he not a good fit? We just got his report card in December, and it was good. There were no signs that you were going to ask him to leave. What has he done wrong?"

But we already knew. The school did not know how to

manage a non-neurotypical child. This time the learning curve was quick. They didn't have to teach him; it was a private school. It took me a bit more time to fully understand that mainstream private schools do not always have the resources to work with students like Michael, and that it is their lawful choice. Applications for other private schools were due in less than two weeks. I was new to the case manager job, but I switched into action mode immediately. That week I looked at five or six other schools, filled out applications, and dragged Michael around to interviews that completely baffled him.

Kids on the spectrum struggle with transitions, even small ones. They struggle to shift gears from being indoors to being outdoors, from a school day to a weekend, from the school year to the summer. Switching schools is a significant change. It was Michael's second year at this school, where he had begun in preschool. We had been unlucky because he'd had two teachers, one okay but new and the other bossy and mean. It hadn't been a great fit, but Michael had been doing okay. There had been no issues or phone calls home. There had been no warning that he was going to be asked to leave. Now, halfway through kindergarten we needed to find a place to start over. We searched and toured and interviewed and applied. Eventually we settled on Wood School, the local public elementary school.

The frenzied week I spent jumping from school to school was like a crash course in elementary school placement. Many of the questions I had expected to ask the schools felt less relevant given the situation, and I was not yet well-versed at articulating all the new questions I had: What kinds of "resources" were available at the school? What was the student-teacher ratio? Was the student body ... diverse? I didn't know how to ask, "Will you be able to give my child with Asperger's a good education?" I was too scared to say the word *autism* for fear I would lose whatever chance we had at getting accepted. What were my legal rights? What kind of protection from discrimination did we have?

After going in circles for what felt like an eternity, we felt optimistic about public school. We planned for Michael to be in the public-school system until college.

Public Versus Private Schools

There are pros and cons to private or public schools for your child with Asperger's. For example, many private schools don't offer accommodations for students with disabilities, and legally they do not have to. Some private schools, on the other hand, do have special services; these schools are extremely expensive but can end up being much more socially inclusive for students on the spectrum. Private schools with these services are hard to find, but they are becoming more common.

We did not find a match like this for Michael. We needed both academics for gifted students and social skill training for challenged students. That combination didn't exist in our state. Furthermore, public schools have access to state and federal funding allocated for kids on the autism spectrum. On the other hand, I do know of students who have been sent to special private schools for Asperger's and other disabilities; in some cases, the public schools had to pay after failing these students. However, strengthened social skills training at special private schools for autism often comes with a tradeoff. The academics might be watered down or need to be supplemented with tutoring. In general, it seems there is no perfect solution (yet) to the education gap for children with autism like Michael.

Every child has different needs, so this decision will differ for every family. As you make your school selection, make sure to weigh the pros and cons in the following areas: school policies regarding disability rights, allocated resources for autism, privacy rights regarding disclosure of disability, past experience with students on the spectrum (and specifically with Asperger's), and staff and administration training and knowledge regarding Asperger's and education.

You might find that the school you anticipated selecting isn't a good match for your child. Enter the school selection process with an open mind. It is all about fit. This is an evolving process and should be monitored. A good match can change with an administration switch or an incompetent teacher. Nothing stays the same, and each year can bring new boons or challenges.

Because we chose public school for Michael, this chapter will be more informative about the public school experience. However, I hope the following tips that I've picked up along the way will be useful to you in any educational setting.

Learn the Lingo

My first piece of advice is that in order to utilize available resources, you need to first learn what they are and how to ask for them. Like any specialized subject, autism comes with its own vocabulary. It's likely that when your child is first diagnosed, you don't speak much of this language. It's time to learn it! Within the school system, the first thing to learn about is an IEP. An IEP is a program devised by you, your school's administration, and disability services in which everyone agrees on the best plan and method to meet the needs of your child and to set long-term goals. This is a legal tool, a form of written advocacy, and something your public school is legally bound to provide.

Depending on your school, getting your child onto an IEP can prove challenging. This is usually because only certain disabilities qualify. Do your research. Let your doctor weigh in on what he or she believes would be best for your child, too.

When you are first learning about the school system, language can sneak up on you and catch you unaware. This happened to me when Michael was in second grade. I was at a team meeting at the school when the principal suggested that Michael be moved from an IEP to a 504 because of his need for minimal academic accommodations. I was barely familiar with a 504 and I didn't know the differences between the two. In reality, while the two plans may seem similar, an IEP must provide the child's current level of school based performance, and specific needs based goals and services, which are evaluated annually. There are no standard requirements or a standard form for a 504. It only provides accommodations and specifies who will provide them.

The school suggested that a 504 was just as good and

said that because Michael was doing well academically, he really didn't need to be on an IEP. I felt like the school was trying to appeal to me by praising Michael for having such a slight disability that he didn't really need to receive any resources for it. Though I felt tempted to agree (I also wanted to believe my son could succeed in school without additional resources), I held my ground and waited to decide until I had consulted with Michael's doctor.

I learned from Dr. Daniels that if I had agreed to get off the IEP and onto a 504, it likely would have cost me $10,000 and a significant legal battle to move Michael back to an IEP. This was when I learned the legal terminology to "stay put." Invoking "stay put" means remaining on your current IEP when questions or difficulties arise in making changes or updates to your child's IEP. When, I told the principal that I wanted to invoke "stay put," I noticed her kick the head of special needs under the table, and I could tell that I had learned something they wished I didn't know. As much as everyone claims to be on the same team at these meetings, you are your child's main advocate. Knowing the lingo and how and when to use it is crucial to successful advocacy.

Neuropsychology Testing

The key to obtaining an IEP is getting a letter with the Autism Spectrum Disorder diagnosis placed in your child's school record. (If your child has another disability, the same rule applies, from hearing impairment to ADHD. You *must* get a letter from your doctor to start receiving services.) Your child also needs to go through educational or neuropsychological testing.

Here, again, you have a couple of options. If you are eligible, with an IEP, public schools will provide this testing for free, but you will be bound to using their tester and their results. Being tested by the school often means waiting, and the reports tend to be less detailed. You can also pay for private neuropsychology testing. The price is steep, typically three to five thousand dollars, but it also means you will receive a more detailed report from an independent source and may have more agency over the wording of it. I would recommend the private testing route if possible. You can apply for public subsidies that will reimburse you for some of the cost.

Michael has been through neuropsychological testing three times. The first was for his initial diagnosis at age four. The second was in eighth grade, and the third was in eleventh grade. All three tests were for different reasons, and we hired a new neuropsychologist each time (although not necessary). Hiring a professional advocate can help you find a good neuropsychologist. These tests are critical to getting your child the resources he or she will need, from elementary school through college.

Neuropsychological tests provide a basis for extended time on exams and standardized testing, accommodations to course work (ie, changes to how your child is taught), homework modifications (ie, changes to what your child is taught), and occupational therapy, among other things. These tests provide the evidence that you, and possibly your advocates or lawyers, will need down the road to guarantee your child the best possible future. As always, the school will be there to offer thoughts and guidance, but it is always best to supplement this knowledge with additional research and objective perspectives. The school's top priority is the well-being of the school, which isn't always the same as the well-being of your child.

When possible, third-party testing can offer the most objective results. Make sure the person you choose is willing to provide a report in a timely fashion after the testing (within a month or six weeks) and is open to discussing the report and making changes if necessary. Ask these questions ahead of time, even if it feels awkward. Divide the payment for the testing between an upfront deposit and a final payment upon receipt of a satisfactory document. Ultimately, the results of your child's neuropsychological tests will have long-lasting repercussions.

Higher Education

Though Michael faced significant challenges in elementary, middle, and high school, it was in college that we felt the available resources drop away. There are, hands down, far fewer resources than there should be when it comes to autism in college.

Michael attended Ivy League school number one, Ivy League school number two, and a third Ivy League quality school for a semester between the two and had a drastically different experience at each. Each school was somewhat equipped to support the special needs students they enrolled, but none was truly prepared to provide a great education for a child on the spectrum.

Witnessing Michael navigate the challenges of his college career ultimately motivated me to become an advocate for future college students with autism. The truth is, many kids on the spectrum do not attend college, and of those who do, many don't graduate. I am working to turn these numbers around.

I founded an organization to help parents advocate and to help fill a major resource gap. My goal was to break down one of the key barriers to success for children on the spectrum. In today's world, a college diploma is a gateway to an independent life. My goal is to be a resource for parents and their children when they have reached the college stage, completed high school, or are trying to figure out the next step.

Looking Back

The day Michael graduated from Ivy League school number two, my role changed. After college graduation I was not going to be on the phone with Michael's teachers or administrators anymore. I would be spending less time (and money) interacting with lawyers, talking to advocates, and pleading with guidance counselors. Michael's college graduation was symbolically, if not literally, a significant step toward his independence.

Looking back over Michael's entire school career, from nursery school through college, I am struck by a few realizations, the biggest of which are the importance of keeping

open channels of communication and trying to find advocates and mentors within the school system. When people—
be they principals, teachers, guidance counselors, deans,
lawyers, advocates, other students, or other parents—truly
understand your child and his or her needs, they rarely stand
in the way of your child's success.

So many of the conflicts we faced arose from fear or a
blind insistence on following rules that were developed with
different circumstances in mind. Some people were afraid or
not invested enough to go out on a limb for Michael. There
was concern with precedent and not making colleagues look
bad by going above and beyond. Administrators don't want to
make exceptions that haven't been made before. Developing
allies within the school system gave us a better chance to
succeed. By having honest and frank conversations with the
people whose cooperation we needed in order to see Michael
succeed, he did.

The other fascinating discovery for me is that rigidity,
which was a big part of who Michael was, seems to have a
brighter implication. It is as if the other side of rigidity was
resilience. On the negative side, Michael was so rigid that
he often said no to a proposed solution simply because he
had already made up his mind. He wasn't open-minded or
flexible. But on the positive side, that same rigidity made
him persevere through high school and college when others
would have given up. He took seven classes a semester at Ivy
League school number two and had to petition every semester to go over the limit. He had to discuss this regularly with
his advisor, as well as with others who feared he would fail.
He advocated and won. I often asked Michael why he hadn't

chosen an easier path, to which he would reply, "I want to get all I can out of my college experience."

If I have any advice on how to navigate your child's school experience, it is to stay one step ahead of playing defense. The worst place to be is trying to dig yourself or your child out of a crisis. It is much easier to try to foresee and avoid the crisis than to end it once it's started. If a good day is one when you don't need to call a lawyer, then a great day is one when you manage to take actions in advance to avoid a potential fire before it even sparks.

Learning the system inside and out will mean having the ability to educate others in the ways that they can be helpful to you and your child. Learn the system, learn the lingo, be involved, advocate. When it feels impossible, remember that it isn't. Take some self-care time to reboot when you need it. Above all else, however, try to remind yourself of the knowledge I wish I'd had: There is always the possibility of a future better than the one you are imagining. It is too easy to convince yourself of the opposite.

The negative experiences Michael went through in his years at school have shaped who he is today. The positive experiences, however, beat out the rest. They gave Michael the tools and strength he needed to become the independent adult he is today. These tools have given Michael the adaptability to embrace his new life and his new self, and the resilience to persevere, learn, and succeed both socially and at work. If we hadn't pushed our way through the muck, we would never have come out on the other side.

Chapter 7
Managing the Legal System and Finances

No parent wants to have lawyers involved in his or her kid's childhood. Neither do we want extra costs to crop up in addition to the already costly adventure of childrearing. Unfortunately, having a child on the spectrum increases the cost of raising a child, and it is important to know and plan for this. There also might be times when your child needs legal assistance, especially for interactions with schools. In this chapter, I will give you a brief run-through on how to manage your legal needs, as well as the costs you can anticipate, which will allow you to plan accordingly.

Legal System—The Players

Lawyers and advocates are the two main players you will go to for advice regarding the legal system, often having to do with your child's education. Lawyers—those wonderful people who went to law school so that you don't have to—are the professionals you can retain and turn to anytime you need someone to navigate the law to ensure your child's rights are being met.

Professional advocates—not to be confused with your child's champions, mentors, or other informal advocates— are people who are well versed in autism, the school system, and to some degree the legal system. You may hire them to attend meetings with you and so they can be available to give advice and support to ensure the best future for your child. However, they are not lawyers and therefore might have limited knowledge on federal laws and state regulations that impact kids on the spectrum from elementary school through college.

How Do I Know If I Need a Lawyer? How Do I Get One?

The most honest answer to this question is that you'll know you need a lawyer when you need a lawyer. Of course, there are certain tip-offs you can look out for. If the police are called or anyone threatens to call the police in connection with your child, it is a good idea to at least speak with a lawyer. If the school is trying to make any significant changes to your child's IEP that you don't agree with, you may need a lawyer. If any serious disciplinary action is taken against your child, you should consider contacting a lawyer. If your child is not making appropriate progress in school or at his or her grade level, a lawyer can help you figure out your legal rights and the options available to you.

Again, there is no set rule about when a lawyer needs to be involved. That said, I found it very useful to keep a lawyer on retainer so that I had someone I knew—and who I knew would be available—should any issue arise. Issues, unfortunately, can and do come up. Not every kid on the spectrum needs legal intervention, but many benefit from legal counsel.

To find a good lawyer who is knowledgeable in autism, I suggest asking for recommendations from parents in your area. I would avoid hiring a lawyer who is not familiar with autism—regardless of how good his or her reputation is—because you will end up spending quite a lot of money simply educating him or her in addition to the cost of whatever services you initially needed. Once you have found a lawyer both you and your child connect well with, hang onto him or her. Build a relationship and keep him or her on retainer so you only have to go through this process once.

Finances—What Are the Costs?

In this book, I've mentioned many costs associated with raising your child on the spectrum. There are not only legal fees but also costs for school, occupational therapy, neuropsychology testing, and psychotherapy. How significant are they? Without going into too much detail, and keeping in mind that costs will differ by geographical area, the following are some general breakdowns.

Legal fees (talking to a lawyer) run from $300 to $750 per hour. School fees depend completely on the school you choose. From the cost of real estate taxes or rent to qualify to attend a public school, to more than $100K a year at the costlier private schools, school expenses come in a wide variety. Occupational therapy costs can also range but will likely fall somewhere around $150 an hour. Educational testing can be free through the public-school system, but private neuropsychology testing can cost upwards of $4,000. Psychotherapy can cost just a small copay of $25 each visit if you are lucky enough to find a therapist covered by your insurance. If not, prices vary, with the top end around $300-$700 an hour depending on the doctor and the city.

The most significant expenditure, however, which is also the most difficult to quantify, is parental time. If I were to hazard a guess, I would say that when focusing on a particular issue for Michael, I would spend between five to forty hours per week. For me—and this will differ from parent to parent—the time required was significant enough to leave my job and focus full-time on my children.

Because every family's financial reality is different, I don't have specific advice on how to manage the burden of these expenses. However, I will say that planning for the costs and time makes a huge difference. If you know what's coming down the road, it's easier to avoid getting hit.

Where to Look for a Break

While planning ahead can be useful for easing the burden of financial hardship associated with autism, it doesn't solve everything. Fortunately, there are also some public resources available to help alleviate costs. Talk to local parent organizations and autism associations in your area to see what public financing is available. Check with your health insurance company to find any coverage you may have overlooked. Check if you can put together a special needs trust; there are laws to help parents who have children on the spectrum do so. Consider public schools as a way of maximizing public funding and limiting costs.

Again, every family's circumstances are different, but there are many options to get your child the best care possible.

Chapter 8
Autism in the Professional World

Each time Michael cycled through a special interest, I permitted myself a bit of imagination: I pictured his obsession becoming a career. When his love of cooking took hold, I imagined little Michael the chef taking the culinary world by storm. When it was making Silly Putty and playing with blocks, I imagined him becoming a sculptor. With his Martin Luther King Jr. obsession, he became an activist and a historian. With easel painting, he was the next Picasso, and with computers he was the twenty-first century's Steve Jobs. Of course, most of the time, the obsessions were just perseverations. He would focus on them acutely before dropping them and moving on. After watching Michael cycle through so many interests, I wondered what he would choose as a career. Would he ever "settle down" and choose something that would captivate him as an adult?

In this chapter, I want to connect the dots of Michael's entrepreneurial history from middle school through his actual debut in the professional world. For so much of Michael's childhood and adolescence, the idea that he might one day have a job and live independently felt like a far cry from reality. Now that he is working and successful in his job, it's hard to believe it felt so impossible early on.

This year, as if to offset any doubt he might still have had about his performance at Apple, Michael received a significant raise on top of an already impressive salary for someone straight out of college. It often still feels like a dream, but then I consider how many other people like Michael there are in his field. He is not as much of an outsider in the tech world as people often made him feel back home. Places like San Francisco and Seattle have proven somewhat safe spaces for young professionals with Asperger's.

The most important message I want to get across in this chapter is that, as parents of children with autism, we can lose hope or let our standards drop in terms of what is possible. Don't talk yourself out of believing in your child's potential. Don't let the fear of failure prevent you from encouraging your child to push and stretch his or her abilities. Michael's path to a rewarding career in data science was not a straight one, and it was never certain. In fact, there were so many roadblocks that sometimes I forgot the road could even be taking him somewhere.

Let this chapter serve as a reminder that every road is heading to a destination, even if it is taking a roundabout path. Let your imagination take off when you think about what your child might one day accomplish.

Starting Small

Michael's professional experience began in middle school with the help of his very creative yet pragmatic guidance counselor. After expressing my concerns to her about the free time Michael had on his hands because of lack of inclusion in after-school programs, she got busy brainstorming. At her suggestion, Michael started tutoring his peers.

It began with just the occasional after-school tutoring session, but Michael surprised us all with his natural teaching ability. His vast knowledge and high intellect, paired with his logical thinking, gave him a gift for painting a clear picture of whatever concept he was teaching. Michael also discovered he had a large reserve of patience and could explain concepts again and again, and in different ways, when necessary. He was not bothered by the kind of repetition with which his neurotypical peers may have struggled. The realization of a new ability was wonderful for Michael. It lifted his spirits and made him feel useful and like he had a higher purpose.

More than simply mastering a new skill set, tutoring gave Michael an additional identity. His peers now saw him in the context of someone who could help them. They saw him as someone with skills different than their own. They saw his intellect and his abilities. This small start, this open door to the world of work, gave Michael a new understanding of himself and what he could accomplish. It was a few years before he further developed those skills, but simply nourishing them at a young age made a big difference.

Growing a Vision

It was in high school that Michael realized he could earn money with his talents. He expanded his client base and began offering private lessons to his peers. With the challenging backdrop of his high school and the bullying that came with it, having an outlet to earn money, utilize his own skills, and interact positively with his peers was a huge boon. Michael loved the fact that some of the same kids who had shunned him in the halls desperately needed him around exam time.

Most of all, Michael actually enjoyed watching other students grapple with and then grasp a concept that had previously been out of reach for them. Beyond just understanding the content he was teaching, Michael had to learn how other people processed their thoughts and understanding. For example, if Michael tried to teach a chemistry concept in one way and it didn't work, he learned that he could approach it in a different way and might be successful. This practice in transitioning between thoughts and methods was a huge breakthrough for us. Michael's tutoring job not only gave him wonderful and transferable professional skills, but it also enhanced his skills in listening and relating to others. This was a double boon.

Broadening Horizons

Even though Michael was a successful tutor, he still felt that his time was underutilized. In fact, he felt underappreciated in a broader sense. High school bullying really took its toll, and Michael's depression was serious. When things felt particularly bleak, I began searching for alternative ways for him to spend his time. I learned about a charity fair, and we went to see if there were any organizations for which Michael might be interested in volunteering. I was surprised when Michael expressed an interest in Samaritans, a charity that provides emotional support to those in need, often those with suicidal thoughts. A friend of mine from college had been involved with Samaritans and had loved it. I mentioned his experience, indicating to Michael that he personally might also find it meaningful. Michael signed up and started with the intensive training that everyone must complete before getting accepted as a volunteer.

Volunteering with Samaritans was all about empathy—something that was not Michael's strong suit—so I was concerned initially about the training and if Michael would pass the test phone call required to join the support team. At first he struggled and needed extra help to master the practice calls. His first test call did not go well enough to pass, but Michael persevered. He felt determined that empathy was something that could be learned with enough practice, so practice he did. The head of Samaritans was kind and gave Michael a second test call opportunity. He passed. After that, Michael had a three-hour shift every Sunday. He answered calls and listened as people talked through their hardships. I could not believe that my son, who had still not figured out how to make meaningful friendships, was succeeding in being an emotional buoy and safety net for those in need of support.

The benefits were really twofold: It was good for Michael to hear about other people's emotional struggles and their battles with anxiety. Helping other people with their problems gave Michael a clearer mind about his own. In addition, it gave Michael something to do on Sunday afternoons. Ultimately, he became a strong and reliable Samaritan. The experience lifted his self-esteem, gave him a new skill set, and gave him the confidence and strength to push through the rest of his challenging high school years.

Had Michael asked me when he was in middle school whether or not I would expect him to volunteer for a suicide hotline, I probably would have said no. I wish I could say that I was always confident that my son could accomplish anything, but the truth was that I had grown used to many of Michael's limitations and was unsure that he could outgrow them or learn how to move beyond them. I'm not even sure it occurred to me that empathy could be a learned skill to the extent it needed to be for Samaritans. As usual, I learned an enormous amount just from watching Michael's skills grow and develop. I was more curious than ever to find out what line of work he would go into. I had to wait at least four more years to find out.

The Big Break

At Ivy League school number one and then at Ivy League school number two, having a job was not really an option. Michael could hardly get his work done, let alone try to carve more hours out of the day.

Even upon graduation, Michael struggled to motivate himself to look for a job. His self-esteem was low and his fear of rejection, high. In a somewhat surprising and fateful turn of events, it turned out that Michael had an acquaintance at Ivy League school number two who was a big fan of his academic skills. He knew Michael was talented, and he didn't want him to let those talents go to waste. This student handed Michael's resume out to recruiters at school. It was thanks to this that Michael received a phone call inviting him to New York for an initial interview with Apple, which eventually led to his job offer.

The day we arrived in San Francisco, the fall after his college graduation, was bright and sunny with clear cool air. It felt like a good omen. I helped get Michael set up in his apartment. We got him settled, having no idea what to expect or how long it would last. Michael has been living there alone successfully ever since—for more than two and a half years now.

The Workplace

As much as this felt like a miracle transition, Michael is still Michael, and he struggles with many of the same challenges in San Francisco that he has struggled with throughout his life. Apple promised him a peer mentor, but this person did not turn out to be very valuable for Michael. The nuances of interoffice dynamics are not easy, and Michael struggles in his interactions with some coworkers who are significantly older and have little in common with him, as well as with his supervisor. He told me that team lunches involve long discussions about "mowing the lawn" and buying appliances for a new home. Obviously, since he does not yet own his first home, Michael has little to add to the conversation and is disinterested by it. However, he is learning every day.

Michael has accomplished things professionally that I never thought would be possible. He has given hour-long presentations in person and via webinars to audiences of more than fifty people. His unique mind is finally being put to good use most of the time.

Having friends in San Francisco has made a huge difference for him. He is now able to ask other people his own age and working in his own field for advice about work and social problems. He has learned that people seem to care about physical appearance, which has prompted him to lose a hundred pounds, become intentional in his clothing choices, go to the gym regularly, and maintain good personal hygiene habits.

One aspect of Michael that was true in college and continues to be true to this day is his strong desire to be challenged. While a neurotypical student might enjoy the break of an easy class, Michael suffers from a refusal to sit through anything too easy. This quality has only increased in the professional world. Michael is happiest at work when he has a meaningful project, can make a difference, and is rewarded for a job well done. While this might be true of many of us, it is heightened for Michael. Something like teleworking, which his employer allows and many of his colleagues delight in, can feel boring and unfulfilling to Michael. It also frustrates him to have too little work to do, and he prefers a clear structure.

At the end of the day, however, Michael is largely satisfied with his field of data science. He keeps his eyes open for new and better opportunities and is constantly approached by recruiters from companies all over the country. I feel profoundly lucky to be able to write these lines. They are not something I ever anticipated being able to say.

If there is one message that has never faltered, it's that a life with Asperger's is a life with hope. Parenting Michael has been full of surprises. The fact that he lives on his own on the other side of the country and works independently at a top Fortune 500 company is a surprise that I never could have imagined. Happy surprises do happen when you have a kid on the spectrum. Don't forget that it is possible to be pleasantly surprised.

Chapter 9
Upending the Downward Spiral

The Downward Spiral

Any parent of a child with Asperger's is likely familiar with the downward spiral. There has been a lot of research done about this, especially when it comes to depression. The downward spiral can be serious or minor. It can last for a few weeks or months, or it may go on for years.

In middle school, when Michael first became aware of his own social limitations, his first minor downward spiral began. "Downward spirals occur because the events that happen to you and the decisions you make change your brain activity. If your brain activity changes for the worse, it contributes to everything snowballing out of control, which further exacerbates your negative brain changes, and so on."[4] I believe Michael's loneliness and his frustration over his own inability to make friends sparked these negative brain changes. The bullying he experienced sparked even more, and the spiral began.

While in the trenches, dealing with the day-to-day issues (juggling school and after school schedules, trying to create weekend plans, attempting to make friends, managing ongoing detentions and school IEP meetings, advocating for change, etc) it's not easy to see the clear picture. I believe it was from this murky, stilted vantage point that we first perceived Michael's state of mind. A small negative event would happen (bullying, exclusion from a social event, an unrequited attempt at making friends) and Michael would feel its negative impact. He would feel sad or angry, talk about it, and express his frustration or disappointment. At the time, these events felt like they caused small downward spirals. John and I hoped that Michael was mostly bouncing back from them. However, in retrospect, I believe Michael was actually experiencing one long downward spiral from middle school all the way until the end of college.

"The big problem with the downward spiral of depression is that it doesn't just get you down, it keeps you down. Depression is a very stable state—your brain tends to think and act in ways that keep you depressed."[5] Despite Michael's determination to make friends from middle school through college, his outlook was growing more and more negative. He

[4] Korb, Alex. *Upward* Spiral. Oakland: New Harbinger Publications, 2015.
[5] Korb, Alex. *Upward* Spiral. Oakland: New Harbinger Publications, 2015.

became more cynical about his abilities and about the possibilities the future held. He grew more easily exacerbated by and less resilient to bullying. By his senior year of high school, he had stopped exercising, and by college I believe his brain was fully set in its downward pull.

Michael had his heart set on attending Ivy League school number one all through high school. It was a dream for him, and when he was accepted, it felt like an enormous success. But there was something else present. Looking back, I can see that, because of his depression, Michael was starting to lose hope about the future. It tinged the celebratory air. Michael was trying hard to act and think positively, but his spiral had reached a point that he couldn't help but question whether college could be a positive experience or not.

During his first year at Ivy League school number one, the environment became toxic for him. Any resilience he did have left was put to the test. Michael started Ivy League school number two in survival mode. He was obese, never exercised, slept poorly at best, and had all but given up the goal of making any lasting friends. Michael's spiral was nearing rock bottom, and his brain was telling him that was where he would stay.

I didn't know what was going to happen. I didn't have any role models for this. I didn't have any pertinent book to read that had a happy ending. Nobody said to me, "Don't worry. Michael will move past this phase and be fine." We tried everything we knew. We tried to get him to exercise; we knew the endorphins could lift him out of the depression and turn him around. But he refused.

Even Michael's psychiatrist, Dr. Masserman, told us it

could be nearly impossible to get a kid on the spectrum to exercise, given a negative and rigid mindset. Once I even tried hiring a trainer to come over with his dogs just to walk around the block with Michael. Michael saw right through this and accused me of plotting against him with the trainer to force him to exercise against his will. Nothing worked. I felt that Michael was pretty close to hitting the bottom when the job offer from Apple came along.

The Upward Spiral

Michael's doctors, advocate, and lawyer have each independently asked me the same question: "What do you attribute Michael's change to?" They still press me for details about what happened. They want to understand how someone like Michael could go from being so unhappy and stuck to feeling happy and fulfilled in such a short time span. They want to help turn things around for others who are suffering. I'm still working out the answers myself, but I largely attribute the change in Michael to the idea of an upward spiral as described below. There is not much research on this concept for people with Asperger's, but we witnessed it with Michael.

Michael experienced a profound culmination of positive life changes simultaneously, enough to give him the boost and the acceptance he needed to be lifted into an upward spiral. Watching the change transpire altered my belief in what was possible. I knew negative spirals, like tornados, happened fast and could wreak impressive damage. I was surprised, however, to see that upward spirals happened just as rapidly, resulting in swift and extraordinary change. Success breeds success. Acceptance breeds acceptance. Receiving the job offer from Apple completely changed Michael's belief that no good company wanted to hire him. The fact that he was offered a job even before he had completed his interviews that fateful day in San Francisco made him feel truly special and valuable. The fact that he was offered a more impressive job (data scientist) than the one he had been interviewing for (software engineer) made him feel like his talents were seen and his voice was heard, and like he could contribute important work to the company, which gave him a purpose.

In addition, the job offer was across the country in a new city. Had the offer been in New York City, Michael's negative spiral might have convinced him that life wouldn't be any different living there a second time. In fact, he had said he never wanted to return to NYC, given his experience. A place as far away as San Francisco, on the other hand, really gave him a sense that he could start over.

The burden of anxiety about having no direction after college was also finally lifted. The fact that a friend of Michael's believed in him enough to hand out his resume suddenly sank in as someone caring for him.

Next came the move to San Francisco: Independence and a positive start. Michael went to San Francisco with the sincere drive to make a good impression, and he did. He learned that his impression became more positive if he had good hygiene habits. He learned that people responded to him better if he was healthier and less overweight. This pushed him to work out, which in turn gave him more endorphins, likely boosting his serotonin levels.

Suddenly Michael was making friends and socializing at and outside of work. He was also waking up for work and going to bed and actually sleeping. He was living on a daily schedule of sleep, work, and exercise, combined with healthy eating and socializing. He also knew that he was far enough from home that he had to figure things out on his own. He didn't have people like his parents to rely on. He was forced to be independent. If this isn't a perfect illustration of an upward spiral, I don't know what is.

I can't help but wonder if it would have been possible for Michael to access this upward spiral sooner. If he had been neurotypical, I think it would have been easier, but rigidity makes the already hard-to-budge state of depression further immoveable. Had I fully understood the extent to which an upward spiral was possible, I would have looked further outside the box for even more ways to help Michael spiral upward.

How can acceptance come sooner? How can a kid develop self-esteem sooner? Was the downward spiral necessary to lead to an upward spiral? I don't think so, but I do believe the contrast between feeling like an outcast for more than ten years and then suddenly becoming a star was magical for Michael. I want every parent of a child on the spectrum to be beyond hopeful; I want parents to feel the true sensation of optimism. Upward spirals exist not only for your average kid but for kids on the spectrum, too.

Three years ago, Michael was a brilliant young adult on the autism spectrum with an Ivy League degree who was at times overcome by depression. There are too many others out there like Michael who never get beyond rock bottom. Let Michael's story be the success story for you that we never had. I hope that this story will guide and motivate you, as well as inspire the sincere belief that the future is bright. There is a whole other world out there on the other side of despair. We found it, and so can you.

Epilogue

Michael lives a good life. He has lived in San Francisco for two and a half years. He boards the shuttle to Apple on weekday mornings around eight thirty or nine, and he leaves work in the afternoon between four thirty and five to head back to his apartment.

He has regular social plans. He goes out to dinner with friends multiple times a week at many of the wonderful restaurants in his local neighborhood and all over the city. He used to eat only chicken and shrimp but now eats all kinds of seafood and food from every culture. He goes to movies and attends concerts, comedy shows, and lectures. Each day he goes to the gym, where he works on new goals. He hikes and bikes for miles. He travels with friends to places like Vancouver, Portland, New York, and Denver.

Michael is recruited regularly by other companies looking for data scientists. He enjoys his job and his colleagues. He likes to be pushed and to feel that his work is meaningful. Michael's looks are strikingly different now. He is in shape and well groomed. I secretly hope he will find his soul mate one of these days—any mother's dream. Of course, these things can take time.

Michael can be a perfectionist, and though much more flexible than he once was, he still has a tendency toward rigidity and hyperfocus. While his looks have changed, the cadence of his speech is still unique. He has not yet agreed to see a therapist regularly in San Francisco, but I have high hopes that this will change.

Michael can be hard on himself. He holds himself to very high standards and is frustrated if he doesn't meet them. For someone so young, he earns an impressive salary. He successfully manages his own finances and personal life. While Michael and I still speak on the phone regularly—almost daily—I only see him in person about three times a year. I miss him, of course, and I hope that one day he will have a job closer to home. Mostly, though, I am so happy to see him thriving.

Michael has been an inspiration to me and to many people who have known him since he was a child. His resilience, brilliance, and intellectual curiosity are fantastic. Michael is also a lot of fun. He has a wonderful sense of humor, and he is full of life and has a sense of adventure. Watching Michael grow up and turn into the adult he is today has been a testament to faith and forward thinking.

Michael inspires the hope of a good and happy life for individuals with the diagnosis of autism.

Appendix 1

DSM IV Criteria for Asperger's Disorder

A. Qualitative impairment in social interaction, as manifested by at least two of the following:
   1. Marked impairments in the use of multiple nonverbal behaviors such as eye-to-eye gaze, facial expression, body postures, and gestures to regulate social interaction
   2. Failure to develop peer relationships appropriate to developmental level
   3. A lack of spontaneous seeking to share enjoyment, interests, or achievements with other people (e.g., by a lack of showing, bringing, or pointing out objects of interest to other people)
   4. Lack of social or emotional reciprocity
B. Restricted repetitive and stereotyped patterns of behavior, interests, and activities, as manifested by at least one of the following:
   1. Encompassing preoccupation with one or more stereotyped and restricted patterns of

interest that is abnormal either in intensity or focus

2. Apparently inflexible adherence to specific, nonfunctional routines or rituals

3. Stereotyped and repetitive motor mannerisms (e.g., hand or finger flapping or twisting or complex whole-body movements)

4. Persistent preoccupation with parts of objects

C. The disturbance causes clinically significant impairment in social, occupational, or other important areas of functioning

D. There is no clinically significant general delay in language (e.g., single words used by age two, communicative phrases used by age three)

E. There is no clinically significant delay in cognitive development or in the development of age-appropriate self-help skills, adaptive behavior (other than social interaction), and curiosity about the environment in childhood

F. Criteria are not met for another specific Pervasive Developmental Disorder or Schizophrenia[6]

---

[6] American Psychiatric Association. *Diagnostic and Statistical Manual of Mental Disorders, Fourth Edition*. VA: American Psychiatric Association Publishing, 2000.

Resources

This book is intended to be a guide for parents and anyone else embarking on or somewhere along the journey of raising a child with Asperger's. It is based largely on my own experience raising my son, Michael, as well as interviews with other parents, teachers, service providers, and college administrators as well as presidents. Throughout Michael's childhood, adolescence, and early adulthood I accumulated many sources that I believe might serve as useful resources for you. This list is not exhaustive, so never give up looking if you don't feel like you've found what you need. Good luck!

Online Resources

Chung, Wendy. "Autism—what we know (and what we don't know yet)." *TEDx Talks*. TED Conferences, March 2014. https://www.ted.com/talks/wendy_chung_autism_what_we_know_and_what_we_don_t know_yet#t-507456.

Magro, Kerry. "The will of opportunity—the path of autism to college." *TEDx Talks*. TEDx Jersey City, March 2015. https://youtu.be/4sg9TlsMRVA.

Shaw, Evelyn. *Early Childhood Technical Assistance Center.* Chappel Hill: ECTA Center, UNC, June 2017. http://ectacenter.org/topics/autism/autism.asp

Books

Attwood, Tony; Grandin, Temple. *Asperger's and Girls: Asperger's women offer candid reflections and the field's leading experts offer advice.* Arlington: Future Horizons, 2006.

Attwood, Tony. *The complete guide to Asperger's syndrome.* London: Jessica Kingsley Publishers, 1998.

Bolick, Teresa. *Asperger syndrome and adolescence: helping preteens and teens get ready for the real world.* Gloucester, MA: Fair Winds Press, 2001.

Bromfield, Richard. *Embracing Asperger's: a primer for parents and professionals.* London: Jessica Kingsley Publishers, 2011.

Elwood, Cornelia Pelzer; McLeod, D. Michael. *Take charge of treatment for your child with Asperger's (ASD): create a personalized guide for home, school and the community.* London: Jessica Kingsley Publishers, 2016.

Grandin, Temple. *The way I see it: a personal look at autism and Asperger's.* Arlington: Future Horizons, 2011.

Greenman, Jan. *Life at the edge and beyond: living with ADHD and Asperger syndrome.* London: Jessica Kingsley Publishers, 2011.

Grossberg, Blythe. *Asperger's rules! How to make sense of school and friends.* Washington, D.C.: Magination Press, 2012.

Hagland, Carol. *Getting to grips with Asperger syndrome: understanding adults on the autism spectrum*. London: Jessica Kingsley Publishers, 2010.

Hudson, Jill; Myles, Brenda Smith. *Starting points: the basics of understanding and supporting children and youth with Asperger syndrome*. Shawnee Mission: Autism Aspergers Publishing Co., 2011.

Jackson, Luke. *Freaks, geeks and Asperger Syndrome: a user guide to adolescence*. London: Jessica Kingsley Publishers, 2002.

Kendall, Craig. *Asperger's syndrome guide for teens and young adults: thriving (not just surviving)*. Visions Publishing, Incorporated, 2009.

Koegel, Lynn Kern; Lazebnik, Claire. *Growing up on the spectrum: a guide to life, love and learning for teens and young adults with autism and Asperger's*. New York: Penguin Books, 2010.

Korin, Ellen S. Heller. *Asperger syndrome: an owner's manual 2 for older adolescents and adults: what you, your parents and friends, and your employer, need to know*. Shawnee Mission: Autism Aspergers Publishing Co., 2006.

Lawrence, Clare. *How to make school make sense: a parents' guide to helping the child with Asperger syndrome*. London: Jessica Kingsley Publishers, 2008.

Lawson, Jackie. *Build your own life: a self-help guide for individuals with Asperger's syndrome*. London: Jessica Kingsley Publishers, 2003.

Ledgin, Norm. *Asperger's and self-esteem: insight and hope through famous role models*. Arlington: Future Horizon, 2003.

Mcafee, Jeanette L. *Navigating the social world: a curriculum for individuals with Asperger's syndrome, high functioning autism and related disorders.* Arlington: Future Horizons, 2003.

Molloy, Harvey; Vasil, Latika. *Asperger syndrome, adolescence, and identity: looking beyond the label.* London: Jessica Kingsley Publishers, 2004.

O'Toole, Jennifer Cook. *Asperkids: an insider's guide to loving, understanding and teaching children with Asperger syndrome.* London: Jessica Kingsley Publishers, 2012.

Patrick, Nancy J. *Social skills for teenagers and adults with Asperger syndrome.* London: Jessica Kingsley Publishers, 2008.

Quinn, Barbara; Malone, Anthony. *Autism, Asperger syndrome and Pervasive Development Disorder: an altered perspective.* Jessica Kingsley Publishers, 2011.

Robison, John Elder. *Look me in the eye: my life with Asperger's syndrome.* NY: Random House, 2007.

Simone, Rudy. *Aspergirls: empowering females with Asperger syndrome.* London: Jessica Kingsley Publishers, 2010.

Volkmar, Fred R.; Wiesner, Lisa A. *A practical guide to autism: what every parent, family member, and teacher needs to know.* Hoboken NJ: Wiley, 2009.

Willey, Liane. *Asperger syndrome in adolescence: living with the ups, the downs and things in between.* London: Jessica Kingsley Publishers, 1999.

Yoshida, Yuko. *How to be yourself in a world that's different: an Asperger syndrome study guide for adolescents.* London: Jessica Kingsley Publishers, 2012.

References

American Psychiatric Association. *Diagnostic and Statistical Manual of Mental Disorders, 5th Edition: DSM-5.* Washington, DC: American Psychiatric Publishing, 2013.

American Psychiatric Association. *Diagnostic and Statistical Manual of Mental Disorders, 4th Edition: DSM-4.* Washington, DC: American Psychiatric Publishing, 2000.

Attwood, Tony. *Asperger's Syndrome: A Guide for Parents and Professionals.* London: Jessica Kingsley Publishers, 1998.

Gray, Carol, and Abby Leigh White. *My Social Stories Book.* London: Jessica Kingsley Publishers, 2001.

Korb, Alex. *Upward Spiral.* Oakland: New Harbinger Publications, 2015.

About the Author

Lily Stamford is an author, motivational speaker, and autism advocate. She began her career as an assistant professor at a local business college. Lily graduated from an Ivy League school and received her MBA as well as a doctorate in business administration.

Lily started a business that enables her to advocate for parents whose kids are over the age of sixteen and preparing to go to college or alternative programs. Currently, advocates are mainly focused on students through high school; after high school and in college, students are typically left to fend for their needs on their own. Parents have some power to help, but colleges often do not want their involvement. What is needed are organizations that advise parents and children on topics such as choosing the best school and tailor a plan to help them be successful in school and during their transition to the working world. Lily's vision is to see every student on the spectrum successfully achieve his or her goals and become his or her best self.

Lily Stamford can be reached at lilystamford1@gmail.com.